WILD
THINGS
HAPPEN
WHEN I
PRAY

WILD THINGS HAPPEN WHEN I PRAY

PRAYING PEOPLE INTO THE KINGDOM

BECKY TIRABASSI

ZondervanPublishingHouse
Grand Rapids, Michigan

A Division of HarperCollinsPublishers

Wild Things Happen When I Pray
Copyright © 1993 by Becky Tirabassi

Requests for information should be addressed to:
Zondervan Publishing House
Grand Rapids, Michigan 49530

International Trade Paper Edition ISBN 0-310-38541-5

Library of Congress Cataloging-in-Publication Data

Tirabassi, Becky, 1954–
    Wild things happen when I pray : praying people into the kingdom /
Becky Tirabassi.
    p. cm.
    ISBN 0-310-54930-2 (pbk.)
    1. Prayer. 2. Tirabassi, Becky, 1954–. I. Title.
BV220.T58   1993
242—dc20   92–33627
                                         CIP

Edited by Harold Fickett and Lori J. Walburg
Cover design and illustration by Church Art Works

Printed in the United States of America

93 94 95 96 97 98 / DH / 9 8 7 6 5 4 3 2

To Vicki,
Candice,
Barbara, and
Mom

I love you!

Contents

Foreword

When I first met Becky Tirabassi at one of our Christian Leaders and Speakers Seminars, I immediately felt her special energy and enthusiasm. Becky had been working in youth ministry, but she had a vision to reach the world and motivate people of all ages to pray. She sought advice on polishing her presentation, shifting her ministry's emphasis, and reaching women.

Over the years I have seen Becky progress and mature. I have been proud to be a part of her ministry both as an encourager and as a recipient of her motivation. Due to Becky and her challenge to pray, my husband, Fred, and I now write our prayers daily. We have seen dramatic changes in our personal and spiritual growth since we heeded Becky's advice to make a daily appointment with God. Indeed, wild things happen when Becky prays—and when *we* pray also!

As a result of Becky's influence, we in turn have encouraged thousands of men and women to come to the Lord daily through written prayer. As you read *Wild Things Happen When I Pray,* I know that you, too, will catch Becky's excitement for God. As you begin to spend time in prayer, you will find that "wild things" do happen. You will discover a God who is real, who is there for you, and who answers prayer!

A couple of years ago I had the privilege of being on the same program as Becky at the Southern California Women's Retreat. Becky spoke before a packed audience of nearly one thousand women. She told her story and challenged the women to pray, and more than half of the women raised their hands in a commitment to spend daily time in prayer. I nearly burst with joy as I watched God using Becky to minister to women.

Today, Becky still ministers to youth, but her ministry has grown to include women and men. Her speaking schedule is full months in advance, and she is reaching the world and motivating them to pray.

Don't just read this book. Follow Becky's advice, and you, too, will find wild things happen when you pray!

Florence Littauer
President, CLASS, Inc.
Speaker and author of *Personality Plus,*
Silver Boxes, and *Dare to Dream*

ONE

Too Busy for God

A sinning man will stop praying. A praying man will stop sinning.

—LEONARD RAVENHILL

At one point in my life, I became so busy "serving God," I no longer spent time *with* him. Meetings and unexpected phone calls stole time away from my quiet, planned time with God. My appointment schedule was jammed with people and activities.

Looking back, I can see how sad my spiritual life had become. At the time, though, I felt no guilt, no sense of shame.

I had slipped into the bad habit of reading my Bible and praying in bed late at night. I only talked to God when I had an urgent request; I let him know my needs, but I never listened to him. Used to making my own decisions, I rarely waited upon God for his advice and direction. I even began to pray after the fact for his blessing on my ventures.

I didn't notice this spiritual laziness creeping up on

11

me, because I didn't seem to be terribly out of step with
other Christians—except perhaps with the pastoral staff,
who incorporated God into their every waking hour
because—as I thought—that was what they were
supposed to do!

Slowly, I became aware of my spiritual poverty. The
quiet, growing conviction that I was missing something
that I had once had troubled me. When I really thought
about it, I was able to admit to myself (but certainly to
no one else) that I was lacking the fire or zeal that
prompts one to talk about God; an enthusiasm that—at
least in me—had once been considered somewhere
between enviable and obnoxious to other Christians.

I couldn't remember where or when I had lost this
fire. The idea made me so uncomfortable that I kept
trying to ignore it.

Then in my seventh year as a Christian, at the
fortieth anniversary of Youth for Christ Convention, I
discovered God again.

Now that may—and should—sound unusual coming from a woman who led three Bible studies per week,
ran a Campus Life group, and had a number of one-on-
one appointments with kids! But at that convention, I
suddenly realized a very basic fact: for me, talking *about*
God had replaced talking *to* God.

I began to search my heart, allowing my rush-rush
lifestyle to be exposed, first to myself, and then to God's
Holy Spirit. That search revealed two things: I really
loved God and truly did feel called to a lifetime of
knowing him and serving him, but my time and
priorities did not reflect that love.

In any personal search, once a person accepts what
she finds, she is propelled to make a decision. My desire

that day was simple: I wanted to *do* whatever it would take to know God better.

So I asked myself, "Spending time with God wasn't always such an effort. It didn't used to bore me. What did I do then to make it exciting?" Memories of hours of reading the Bible—and being inspired and motivated by it—flooded my thoughts. I recalled times when I had read verses and allowed them to set off a spark of fire within me, enough to get me up out of a chair and moving. And I remembered how God's Spirit prompted me to share Christ with someone, empowered me to make a decision in a difficult time, or even comforted me emotionally.

Yet, on deeper reflection, I recognized that those sparks and fires and answers had come from purposely putting myself in the midst of God. Confronting myself honestly, I admitted that I had been neglecting a few simple components in my daily walk with God. I knew that hearing or reading the Word moves a person to act in faith. I knew that daily, diligent, concerted prayer fills a person with awe of God. Yet I was cutting myself off from the source of my power when I made myself too busy to meet with God.

This moment of discovery called for a radical response—not a response that was natural or normal, easy or explainable, but a response that was intense and determined and out of the ordinary. I was on the verge of going deeper with God, but at that moment, no one was taking my hand and leading me. Blindly, I reached out my hand to the unknown.

ONE HOUR A DAY

Then Someone took my hand and led me. At that convention, in the presence of just one witness, I prayed, "I want to know you better, Lord. I make a decision to spend one hour a day with you for the rest of my life."

This was no ordinary prayer. In fact, no youth worker in her right mind would knowingly add another one-hour commitment to her already overbooked schedule. Yet it wasn't by suggestion, nor by human prompting, that I made this decision. I felt prompted by God's Holy Spirit. And even though I was aware of the Bible's warnings against breaking a vow, I was not intimidated.

I felt this prayer wasn't to be treated lightly, yet I felt as I did the day I had become a Christian.

First, I had an incredible enthusiasm to tell others that I had made a decision to spend time with Jesus and that my life was definitely going to change because of it. Looking back, I'm grateful no one tried to burst my bubble, suggesting that I was not an ideal candidate for this kind of commitment—although many people have kidded me that with my fun-loving, talkative personality, I seemed the most unlikely person to take on this kind of discipline!

Second, the thought never crossed my mind that I wouldn't be able to keep this promise to God. Just like a new Christian, I didn't see this commitment as burdensome, but exciting. I anticipated the time of reading the Scriptures and praying, just as I had those first few years of my spiritual life. And with that childlike faith came an overwhelming inner renewal that swept away bad habits, poor discipline, and attitudes that had hindered and hampered and hedged out exciting, fruitful times with God.

Third, I never imagined everything that would change, be uncovered, and explode because of this one-hour appointment with the King—just as I never would have believed that my conversion in 1976 would lead to sixteen years of ministry.

Last, I found myself in confession. Longing to return to my baby Christian fervor of loving God—talking, listening, and waiting for him—I acknowledged that my lack of time with him was sin in my life that had been separating me from him, and I purposed to make regular, daily appointments with the King.

But just what was I going to do during those times with God?

MAKING TIME FOR "MY PARTNER"

It was obvious to me that I was not inherently disciplined. I knew that to spend time with God regularly I would need a plan—a plan that would include all facets of prayer and Bible reading.

Within the first few months of my daily commitment to spend one hour a day with God, I asked him for an idea to get me organized. He showed me that what had worked for me in other areas of my life were notebooks to record ideas and conversations, and calendars to schedule appointments and meetings. So I devised a prayer notebook to help me plan my time with God. Little did I know that this simple idea would be one that I would share with thousands of other Christians in the years to come. (Be careful when you ask God for an idea!)

The key was to make the notebook simple and practical. I used the notebook to write my prayers. Written prayer helped me overcome the bad habits I'd developed of daydreaming and getting distracted with other activities. Therefore, journaling my prayers in an organized pattern became part of my daily appointment with the King.

MY PARTNER PRAYER NOTEBOOK

That's how *My Partner Prayer Notebook* was born. It became my tool for praying—or having conversations with God. Writing in my prayer notebook allowed me to express every type of prayer, ranging from confession to thank-you notes to God to pouring out my soul.

To make sure my time with God would be a two-way conversation, I divided the notebook into two sections: My Part in prayer to God, and God's Part in responding to me.

My Part

I use the acronym P.A.R.T. to describe the four different types of prayer that make up my part of my daily dialogue with God.

The *Praise* section is where I record personal praise prayers to God. I actually rewrite or paraphrase four to five psalms a day, in numerical order from 1–150. The psalms, written by those who had a heart for God, are models of prayer that teach me to pray.

The *Admit* section of my notebook is the place where I confess sin to God on a daily basis. Written confession serves two purposes for me: (1) I am more responsible for my actions when I know that I have agreed with God about what I should do, and (2) I am not able to hide things from God when I have committed myself to being honest with him. By meeting with God daily I wasn't necessarily looking for an increase in holiness, but it has definitely been a welcomed result!

The *Requests* section lists all my petitions to God. *Wow* is the first word that comes to my mind when I think about my prayer request list over the past eight years! Exciting answers, incredible changes in lives and circumstances, and great new ideas are all benefits of having and maintaining a prayer request list. No longer can you forget to pray for someone or something if you write it down. No longer can chance or coincidence take credit for God's working in specific response to your requests.

And though some answers may take years—yes, *years*—to be answered, asking, waiting, and watching expectantly are all aspects of a healthy prayer life. And so is accepting "no" as God's best answer for certain requests.

Finally, the *Thanks* section is my place for writing my thank-yous to God. This causes me to consider all that God is doing and has done for me—constantly making me more appreciative and aware of his concern for every aspect of my life.

God's Part

The second part of my notebook contains God's words to me. This section is also divided into several sections: Listening, Messages, New Testament, Old Testament, and Proverbs.

For the average believer, the ability to listen to God

develops with practice. Knowing God and spending time with him enables us to recognize his voice. We would all agree that process takes time. Slowly we will develop a familiarity to God, to the thoughts and nudges that prompt us because they are rooted in Scripture and in his character. As we listen to God in quiet reverence, we submit our inner selves to his corrections, direction, and wisdom. And as we write down what we believe God is saying, he reveals himself to us. With time his voice becomes familiar, like that of a dear friend.

In the message section of my notebook I keep notes that I have taken during sermons or Bible studies. I record thoughts that I had while listening to a radio program or to a conference speaker. Then not only do I remember the message, but God uses the notes to inspire, convict, or prod me into action. Not to mention the fact that it also increases my attentiveness during talks!

The Word of God, if we believe it to be living and active and sharper than any two-edged sword, will radically change our lives—*if we let it!* Therefore, the last three sections of *My Partner Prayer Notebook* have blank pages waiting to be filled with verses from the New Testament, Old Testament, and Proverbs—verses that either convict or comfort me as I am reading them.

Through focusing not only on my part, but also on God's part in our time together, the hour I spend each day with God becomes a time of exciting dialogue with my Creator. Daily, scheduled, written prayer, unlike anything I had experienced up to that point in my Christian walk, led to a new, more mature love for my Friend and Lord, Jesus.

TWO

An Appointment with the King

When a Christian is winning souls, he isn't messing around with sin.

—GEORGE L. SMITH

I rush around each morning making lunches, throw in a load of laundry, and dry a few dishes in order to get a little housework done. Then, once I've gotten the boys off to work and to school, I collect my quiet-time tools—a cup of coffee, a journal, a pen, and a wrist watch—and head out the back door to my favorite lawn chair.

The hour I spend with the Lord is always the best part of my day. I turn the lawn chair to face the sun and settle in. At my left is a little flower garden with stepping stones, to my right is a small lawn, and at my feet are the still, quiet waters of a pool. This is my personal "Psalm 23" setting. Usually so busy, here I allow myself to slow down, reflect, quiet my heart, pour out my soul, and listen to God. The birds sing, insects hum, and cars roar by, but they don't interrupt. Even the sky usually cooperates with blue cloudless days, but when it doesn't,

I start a fire in the living room fireplace to set the mood for my appointment with the King.

BLESSINGS AND RESULTS

Before long, I became aware that those who love the Lord communicate honestly with him. They are obedient to him out of a genuine desire to please him. They are faithful and loyal to him, and find great joy in representing him. And through them others see a God who surprises and delights them. In fact, the more consistent we are in our relationship with God, the more convincing we are to those who are observing.

I noticed that little things, such as the way we drive our cars or the way we treat our kids, will affect how someone else feels about God. From my appointments with God, I gained noticeable stability, strength, and consistency. Instead of trying not to offend people, I began to desire to *please* God.

I had a new and greater motivation to tell others about Jesus. This motivation came, not from being a "good person" so that others would see God in me, but by *living to love him*. That gave me both confidence to share my faith and enthusiasm to live a life right with him!

Because I am committed to spending an hour a day with God, I have had to make my calendar reflect my priorities. The only way—and I've tried them all—that I have gained success in keeping appointments with God is by writing in my calendar, the day ahead, at what time the next day I will meet with God. By committing myself to an appointment, I've decided that nothing else will interrupt or "bump" my time with God.

Writing down my conversations with God, as well as recording his responses to me, has made our time come alive! For over eight years now, I have had daily, one-hour appointments with God. And that's the real proof that an energetic, fairly undisciplined youth worker could successfully change her busy ways!

KNOW HIM BETTER; MAKE HIM KNOWN

If this "appointment with the King" theory sounds overpowering or legalistic, it is not meant to be in any way. I simply believe that one who knows God better will be both compelled and excited to make him known, and will do so with a deep integrity that comes from spending time with him. In fact, because of my personal experience, I'm convinced that evangelism will become second nature when planned appointments with the King have a chance to influence our lives fully.

But, you may be thinking, what of our weaknesses: the fear of rejection, doubt in our ability, or lack of knowledge?

Charles Spurgeon, an Englishman who lived during the reign of Queen Victoria, was called the "prince of preachers." At age fifteen, he became a Christian, and his preaching changed the lives of thousands. Self-taught, he never attended seminary, yet from 1861 until his death in 1892, he preached to six thousand people in London every Sunday!

Knowing how difficult it is to speak boldly about Christ, Spurgeon said, "Speak to God of your inhibitions, self-centered concerns, and fears, and he will replace them with purpose and power." He went on to say, "Be like a conduit pipe, receiving from heaven and delivering to the people what the Lord bestows."

I challenge you: Take his advice. You need not be a preacher or a teacher. All you need to do is simply share the Lord you know and love with the one or one hundred whom God has put into your life, perhaps for that very purpose.

Our deepest motivation for evangelism should be love for God. That love will naturally compel us to learn how to be effective and excited in our witness for the Lord Jesus Christ, and it will encourage us to be prepared at all times, knowing that if we are ready and available, God will use us.

THREE

Prepare with Prayer

Nothing makes us love a man so much as praying for him.

—WILLIAM LAW

One morning, out by the pool, I opened *My Partner Prayer Notebook* to a fresh page. I never know exactly what will happen when I pray, but I've come to expect that wild things happen when I do pray—that's just the nature of prayer!

As I do each morning, I began by reading and rewriting four to five chapters in the book of Psalms, paraphrasing every verse that expresses how I feel. I no longer marvel at the fact that what I read each day in Psalms is truly what I am feeling. Reading Psalms in numerical order, always—not just often or sometimes, but *always*—expresses my thoughts and circumstances. Psalms comforts me and connects me to the Old Testament. I expect God to know where I'll be reading that day and know that he will be there to meet me through those very verses.

Then I went on to the Admit section in my prayer

notebook to agree with God where I've been wrong. (Aah, yes, some days are spent longer here than others. Such is life.)

Hmmm, let's see . . . next came my prayer list. It's usually filled with family members and friends' names for various requests from health to finances to relationships to . . .

Salvation. When I know someone needs the Lord, I prepare for evangelism with prayer. I pray that they will come to know the Lord, and I pray that I will be prepared to talk with them about the Lord, if need be. Today, a woman named Vicki was on the top of that prayer list of people who needed to know the Lord.

A NEW MANICURIST

I had met Vicki just last week. She was my new manicurist. I can't figure out if I'm lazy or vain or just getting old, but having my nails polished and manicured biweekly has become part of my routine.

On Fridays I would teach an aerobics class at a health club on the second floor, then run downstairs to the beauty salon to have my nails done. I always rushed into the salon sweaty, breathless, barely on time, and in a hurry to leave.

That's when I met Vicki for the first time, as her customer. She was quiet, reserved, had long, blondish straight hair, and seemed about my age. Her "station" was bright and businesslike, filled with at least fifty bottles of nail polish, pictures of a recent cruise, her business license, neatly folded towels, brushes, and a lamp.

Within one of our first few appointments, she asked

me what I did for a living. Never shy about what I do (in fact I find it to be a great advantage), I carefully shared that I was a Christian author and speaker to students and adults. I say "carefully shared" because I couldn't tell by her reserved tone of voice if she might take my "Christian talk" as too pushy or not of interest.

But because she would look up at me every so often and nod her head, I gathered that she must be somewhat curious—at least intrigued—so I continued talking.

A WALKING TIME BOMB

"You see," I told her, "when I was fifteen, I wanted to be popular. I just wanted to be liked. In my mind, anyone who drank was cool. And more than anything, I wanted to be accepted, popular, cool.

"I didn't really see drinking as bad or wrong. Both of my parents and a lot of my relatives drank regularly, if not daily. It was kind of a Midwest thing to do, you know?"

She nodded her head as she brushed on the polish. I continued, "The first night I drank was on the Fourth of July, before my first year in high school. I anticipated the buzz, the laughter, and the excitement that would be a part of the night—and it was exactly as I thought it would be!

"I didn't know, though, that I would become a different person when I drank. With just a few beers in me, I wasn't inhibited or quiet around people that I didn't know. In fact, that first night I drank, I went right up to people that I wanted to meet and introduced myself! I had a new boldness or cockiness about me that I immediately liked—and counted on to return. With a little liquor in me, I even told jokes and made people laugh. I could tell people thought I was funny. They'd say, 'You're the life of the party, Becky!' I loved it. It made me feel great to drink. I thought this was popularity! I knew I would do it again.

"And I did. I drank every weekend in high school from that Fourth of July on. At first I drank only after the games or at the parties. Then, as the football season rolled on, we would get our liquor before the games and drink in a van in the parking lot. We drank till we got high, then went in to the game. Eventually, I just went to the games drunk. I never had one or two drinks. No, I drank to get high, to get drunk."

Vicki gave me a look that hinted she, too, had lived in this world at one time, but her quiet manner kept me wondering.

"I was a walking time bomb," I said. "Little did I realize that I was progressing quickly through the stages of alcoholism.

"But I didn't know that then. I simply thought I was having fun and doing what everyone else was doing. I didn't really notice that I was a bigger drinker than most of the guys—and when I did, I just became one of their favorite drinking buddies, not a girl that they wanted to date seriously.

"Soon, alcohol wasn't enough. I started smoking dope and doing Quaaludes, then eventually bootleg speed. I mixed my liquors throughout the day to include beer, wine, and Scotch. I never stopped drinking until I passed out, blacked out, or drove myself home to crash. I was completely addicted to both drugs and alcohol by the time I was nineteen years old—but I would have never told you that I even had a problem."

"I'M AN ALCOHOLIC"

Again, I briefly stopped to gauge if I had shared enough, was talking too much, or if I should continue. Sensing that "go ahead" feeling, I asked, "Should I go on?"

Vicki shrugged and said, "Sure."

So I went on. "My friends changed from the moment I began drinking. My grades dropped, and I began to look like a hard, cold, tough young girl. Still, I continued to drink and do drugs until I was twenty-one.

"The summer I turned twenty-one, my life changed. At the time I was living in California, but I had returned home to Cleveland, Ohio, to be in a wedding. I stayed with my parents that week, but I spent most of my time with my friends. I couldn't wait to tell them about my outrageously wild life in California—and, of course, to brag about my blonde boyfriend.

"That whole week, we drank and drank and drank. Thursday night of the bachelorette party, I had a half of a fifth of vodka with a friend. From that party, at 7:00 P.M., we went to a local bar to dance and continue to party. But that was the last thing I remember. I don't know where I lost or left my friends—or my car—to this day. I only remember waking up next to someone I barely knew at 6:30 the next morning.

"I was in shock. I didn't know where I was or how I got there, what I did with this person or where my friends were. Immediately sick to my stomach, I asked for a ride home. I was so ashamed of myself I couldn't even ask simple questions that would have put the pieces of the previous night together for me.

"But two thoughts pounded my brain. The first

was, *Becky, do you know what they call girls like this?* And the second was, *You would have never done this if you hadn't been drinking.* I knew myself well enough. When I was sober, I would never have gotten myself into a situation like the one I was in.

"As I let myself into my mother's screen door, I wondered, *What have I become?* The first thing I said to my mother were the words, 'Mom, I'm an alcoholic.' No one needed to tell me that I was. No one needed to convince me. I had just convinced—no, proven it to—myself. My life was completely out of my control and under the control of liquor. I knew that day that I was not able to stop drinking. I was almost in shock.

"And so was my mother. She had alcoholic relatives. She knew that members of our family used and sometimes abused alcohol. But now me, her youngest daughter?

"I knew I couldn't drink, but how was I going to avoid the inevitable? It wasn't going to be easy or fun to stay dry, but I never wanted to feel that humiliation or self-hate again. For the rest of that morning I cried tears of regret and embarrassment. Finally, though, I had to pull myself together and go to the wedding rehearsal.

"When I was offered a drink, I almost gagged at the thought of liquor. Whatever I had had to drink the previous night was still in my nose and throat. Nauseated, I just used my hangover as my reason for not drinking, but there sure was pressure from my friends for me to get the party rolling! I would have obliged, but I was afraid to take a drink for fear of what I might do. My friends were almost disappointed, but I assured them that we still had the wedding to enjoy the following night."

I stopped. But I could tell she was waiting for me to go on.

"The following night, the night of the wedding, I decided I would not drink again. The feelings of shame and remorse had not faded one bit. I wished I could say I still had a dull hangover from the bachelorette party, but I didn't have that excuse anymore. Yet there was a growing fear in me that my life would completely race out of control if I took just one—and I knew it would take only *one*—drink.

"My friends all noticed—I wasn't drinking! They couldn't figure it out. They offered me drinks, beers, champagne—they all offered. Finally they asked, 'Why aren't you drinking?'

"I thought I'd break in the newness of my discovery to them, so I said, 'I think I have a drinking problem.'

"They all laughed and patted me on the back. 'You do not, Becky. You're the life of the party! Just slow down,' they all chided. But they didn't understand. I couldn't slow down. I could not have *just one* drink. I knew no limits."

CRUCIFIED ON THE STAND

Vicki changed hands now, but again, simply by her silence, she gave me unspoken permission to continue my story.

"I didn't drink that night at the wedding, but within the next few days, back in California, I began to go through withdrawal. I had everything from anxiety attacks to panic attacks to paranoia, and finally thoughts of suicide began to bombard my mind. I felt like I was having a nervous breakdown on the inside, while on the outside attempting to appear to my friends and co-workers as if I was 'together' and had simply decided to quit drinking. In only three weeks, my world began to crumble.

"A year earlier, while drinking, I had been in a car accident. On my way to the lawyer's office for the unofficial court hearing, I started painfully evaluating my first twenty-one years of life—full of drugs and alcohol, immorality, lying, and even stealing.

"I knew I couldn't take any more. I had come to the end of my rope and I was about to snap. When the lawyer called me alone into his office to prepare me for the upcoming cross-examination, he told me if I lied on the stand, I'd be crucified.

"I looked at him, stunned by his dramatic choice of words.

"The word *crucified* jolted my memory to Easter Sunday of that year. I had attended church, like all good Americans do, you know, and found myself quite 'out of it' with the whole scene. I looked more like a displaced disco dancer than a churchgoer, but I had been raised to go to a liturgical church, and somehow holidays didn't seem complete without attending."

Vicki didn't look up, but she did crack a small smile, and added, "I grew up in that kind of church, too."

SHEER ABANDONMENT

I knew that I was getting to the real exciting, but spiritual part of my story, so I began to talk faster and softer.

"Only the janitor of the little church ventured over to me that Sunday. He tapped my shoulder and called me, 'Sister.' I about crawled under the pew. *I'm not your sister,* I thought. But we exchanged names, and I was certain that I would never see him again.

"I was wrong. Monterey, California had only one mall. There was a bar on the basement level that I went to for happy hour, and a bunch of other stores on the upper levels. Ralph, the janitor, often seemed to find me there! He would say the weirdest things to me, such as, 'Jesus loves you just the way you are.' And I remember thinking, *Buddy, you don't know the way I am, or you would never have said that.* He bugged me. I thought he was a strange Jesus-freak, and I wanted no part of the fellow . . . until that lawyer told me I would be crucified on the stand if I lied. At that moment, I knew I had to find Ralph, the janitor.

"I was about to lose it emotionally and physically. I needed help and Ralph was the only person I could think of who might have the answer to my pain and addiction and despair.

"I was desperate. I knew instinctively I would not make it another day trying to juggle the mental anguish that was oppressing me. I drove directly to the church where Ralph, the janitor, worked. Of all the people and places I could turn to, he seemed the only one who had offered me words of hope.

"I flew down the steps of the church basement to find him. I looked first in the janitor's closet. There I found Ralph in his blue jeans, flannel shirt, and work boots, ready to buff the floors."

With only a short time left in our appointment, I had to keep going.

"I had been crying for over an hour, so my face was

puffy, red, and streaked from tears. 'Ralph,' I pleaded, 'I need to talk.'

"'No, Becky, we just need to pray,' he replied, as if he had been waiting for me to show up at his doorstep one day! We slipped into the junior church room adjacent to the janitor's closet and sat in two little chairs sized for young children. He asked me if I would like to repeat a simple prayer after him, asking Jesus to come into my heart and to forgive me for my sins.

"I did, without any hesitation. It seemed too late to consider the consequences or costs of this prayer. There were no more options in my life. I had lost all that I had ever wanted or dreamed of. I had nothing to hold on to anymore. I was completely willing to ask Jesus into my life, even if it meant—and I hoped it *would* mean— drastic changes. I was ready for God's help.

"I had no idea what would occur from the moment I finished praying. I just needed to get through one day without torment. So, with sheer abandonment, I asked Jesus to come into my heart and forgive me of my sins— and I even named them out loud, every one I could think of! Through my tears, Ralph led me in a prayer, and with childlike faith I asked Jesus to come into my life and make me new.

"Vicki," I continued, "at the close of our prayer, I looked up with a new face, new eyes, no more fear, no more desperation. I felt an unexplainable peace. And in that moment I knew that I was released from the addiction to alcohol. I knew—or better yet, I *believed*— that I was forgiven. I felt lighter, as if the weight of my lifestyle was being lifted off of me because I hated it, I had confessed it as sin, and I was truly sorry."

Vicki stopped me long enough to ask, "How could

you change just like that? I mean, what happened to your friends, your boyfriend?"

I replied, "I knew I had been set free. I had been given another chance. Of the little that I knew of the responsibility of one who knows God, I began instinctively to live as if I loved him and began to tell others everything that had happened!

"It was odd, but even my foul, gutter language completely stopped. I moved out of the apartment I had been sharing with my boyfriend within the week. But most dramatic of all, the desire to have a drink was gone! I was not badgered by those constant, tempting, nagging thoughts about alcohol."

Before she could even ask, I answered her question. "Where did they go? I can't explain that part of my experience, but it was one of the very factors that caused many of my family and friends to become interested in God!"

Time was up! We had discussed way more than I ever thought I would share so soon after meeting. I felt a little awkward, but I offered to bring a book to her with my story in it, if she would like.

"Sure." She smiled.

From what little I knew about Vicki, I wanted her to know how much Jesus loved her. Oh, if she only knew that he could fill her emptiness and give her peace and hope! I knew that he could touch her. I believed he would.

Her overall quietness seemed to reflect some hurt and insecurities, but she hadn't shared them with me yet. But if our relationship was typical of the beauty salon scene, it wouldn't be long before I would know her past, her present, and her future dreams.

FOUR

Dare to Share

I am not ashamed of the gospel, because it is the power of God for the salvation of everyone who believes.
—ROMANS 1:16

I believe my relationship with Vicki developed easily and naturally for two reasons. First, I prepared for my meetings with her by praying. Before I even knew very much about her, I cared about her because I had been praying for her. Second, we developed a friendship because I opened up and told my own story. I dared to share something about myself with someone I barely knew.

Often, in the course of my life and ministry, I've simply told my story in a sentence, five minutes, two hours, or over five months. Rarely have I had to share about doctrine or theology. I don't attribute my success in evangelism to education, but to daring to share what changed my life. Like a leper healed by Jesus, I've run to tell others where they can get help.

Leonard Ravenhill, a powerful writer on prayer and revival, said, "A man with an experience of God is never at the mercy of a man with an argument, for an experience of God that costs something is worth something and does something."

True, it's important to know what and who you believe. But I have found that a personal experience is far more interesting to hear and difficult to refute. As you enthusiastically, confidently, and unashamedly tell your story to a nonbeliever, the strength of your testimony will often bring up a question, comment, or doubt. By that person's comment, you will gain a clue as to where she is in her spiritual journey.

SYLVIA

One night I arrived late back at my hotel room. Feeling hungry, I dialed room service. A woman who introduced herself as Sylvia answered the phone.

"It's late," she said, "but I think we can still make you a fruit salad. I'll try to get you something in the next half hour, if I can."

Her warm, friendly voice reassured me that she would find me dinner, so I settled back in a chair to read. When the knock on my door came at the half hour, I jumped up and ran to open it.

It was Sylvia! Her gold name tag stood out on her black tuxedo. She was as warm and friendly as her voice. But I was surprised to see her at my door, since I remembered that she had taken the order.

She smiled. "You must be a lucky lady!"

"What do you mean?" I asked, returning her smile.

"Well, just look at what the chef fixed for you," she said proudly as she unveiled my plate of fruit.

"Well, I'm a Christian lady . . ." I said slowly, not

wanting to put down her comment about luck, but wanting to let her know that I didn't believe in luck.

"Oh, so you don't believe in luck?" she asked.

I realized she had caught on about me and "luck." I still did not want to offend her, but I did want to share what I really believed in, so I added, "No, but I am a woman of prayer!"

This conversation had escalated into a faith discussion faster than I had ever anticipated. *Where will it go from here?* I wondered.

I didn't have long to wait. Because then she surprised me by asking, "Will you pray for me, Christian lady?"

Suddenly our brief meeting had become very deep. I nodded. Laying my hand on her shoulder, I said, "Let's pray now."

Just before I could bow my head or close my eyes, she said, "I've been looking for God for twenty-five years. I'm Muslim. Do you know what? I think he's right here," she said, pointing to her heart.

I was astounded at the course of our conversation. With rising joy, I prayed out loud with Sylvia, "O Lord, please come into Sylvia's heart. Cause her to know you in a personal way ..."

She looked up at me when I had finished praying. Softly, she said, "Thank you, Christian lady."

LOOK FOR A HOOK

Some of us don't have dramatic personal testimonies—I've often wished I didn't! But we all have ways of showing people we would like to get to know them, be their friends, and help them.

In all of your encounters, then, *look for a hook*. Watch for key words or thoughts, common interests or issues that can lead to an enjoyable conversation and that might give you an opportunity to share your faith. In Sylvia's case, the hook was the small word *luck*. I used that word as a starting point to convey my own beliefs.

How can you find a hook practically, even easily? First, find a common interest to talk about, whether that be children, fitness, age, past experiences, or current hobbies. Ask nonthreatening questions and listen attentively. Soon you will find yourself on common ground.

Then, as you become comfortable with the other person, add a verse or illustration that is meaningful or helpful to the conversation. If you have the opportunity, you can share books and tapes that are relevant to your discussions.

Listen carefully for a natural entrance to share your faith, such as: "It sounds like you're really discouraged. I find as a Christian that talking to God in prayer is a wonderful way to relieve fears and anxieties." Then offer to pray for them, then or later.

The more opportunities and adventures in which you are involved, the more you will increase your effectiveness, boldness, and enthusiasm for sharing your friend, Jesus.

The following three actions, if practiced, will allow you to be natural, not forced, and should create a mutual friendliness.

BE APPROACHABLE

First, develop an approachable personality. Smile. Be kind. Offer assistance. Don't judge a person by his or her outer appearance. Be willing to chat. Say "hello" first. Even reach out to the most hurting or lost or overweight, the handicapped or the unhappy—you may be the first person in a long time to offer someone hope and genuine concern.

BE INQUISITIVE

Second, casually ask the person what she feels or believes about God. Use questions that are easy or natural to ask of a perfect stranger, such as:

- "Have you ever attended church? What type?"

- "Do you attend church now? Do you mind sharing with me why or why not?" (or "Oh, how come?")

- "What are your thoughts about life after death?"

One or more of these questions could create plenty of discussion—if you are a good listener.

Just a note: If you are involved in full-time ministry, you will have to be more careful so as not to appear as if you have an ulterior motive.

BE ALERT

Remember that a Spirit-led boldness will often prod us at unexpected moments. Be aware of those divine appointments that God sets up for you. Even if you resist, God will often keep working. One hectic Sunday taught me that lesson.

Not loving to be alone, sit alone, or ride in airplanes or shuttle buses alone, I tend to make new friends on every trip I take. But this particular Sunday, I had no time to make friends. I had to get off the plane, collect my luggage, grab a taxi or shuttle, and dash to the hotel, where I would check in, get ready for church, and catch a taxi to take me across town. All that in an hour and a half!

My plans fell apart from the onset. First, my plane took off thirty minutes late. Then, when I got to the baggage-claim area, only two of my three bags came off the carousel. Having previously experienced "lost-luggage syndrome," I knew I had one hope to make it to church: Run to the Delta baggage counter and have them call the baggage handlers who unloaded the plane—they could check for my bag before it took off for its next destination. I began to pray like crazy, "Oh Lord, help me, please!"

I ran, talked fast, ran back to the baggage return . . . and sure enough, a lone carry-on bag toppled off the belt. It was mine! I snatched it up and waved to the amazed Delta agent as I dashed off.

Now I was more than fifty minutes behind schedule. As soon as I stepped out into the ground transportation area, I had more timely decisions to make. Spotting a shuttle-bus driver, I hurried over to him. He assured me that the next bus would be departing in five to seven minutes. Hurrah! I hopped on—and proceeded to wait fifteen minutes.

Now I was beginning to grow not only impatient, but angry that I had been misled about the departure time. If I had known about the delay, I could have easily taken a taxi. I left my spacious front-row seat, got off the bus, and questioned the driver once again regarding the estimated time of arrival at my hotel. He assured me I'd be downtown to my hotel in twenty minutes, just barely enough time to make it to church, but I could still do it.

With some reservation, I considered whether to get my bags off the bus and head for a taxi. Slowly I reboarded the bus, only to find my front-row seat occupied. To the back of the bus I headed.

I sat down next to a business-looking woman. I was too preoccupied with trying to meet my schedule to even say hello. I tapped my fingers on the seat ahead of mine, looked at my watch every other minute, and sighed deeply.

Finally, the shuttle door closed and off we went at an excruciatingly slow, southern pace. Just then the driver listed seven hotels he had to stop at. I almost died! Now frustrated, I looked around. The occupants in each set of seats had struck up a conversation, and for once (and it's rare), I didn't even feel like talking. Within a matter of seconds, however, I asked the woman next to me what line of work she was in.

"Sales and marketing," she responded. Then she inquired, "Why are you in such a hurry?"

"Well," I said, "there's this really great preacher in Atlanta, Dr. Charles Stanley, that I've always wanted to hear in person, and I'm only in town tonight. He is on national television and has a radio ministry. I've been looking forward to hearing him, but the service begins at 6:30! I don't want to miss it. He really is a great preacher."

Because of my past experience with conversations like this, I knew that this could make her uncomfortable.

Instead, she asked, "What kind of church is it? What

does he talk about? Why are you so determined to hear him?" I told her about his style of preaching, his monthly magazine, and how encouraging I find his words.

Then, amazingly, she asked, "What hotel are you leaving from? Could I join you?"

As it turned out, the Hilton where I was staying was right across the street from the Marriott where she had a reservation. We planned to meet out front of my hotel at 6:00 P.M.

I was amazed at God's providence. The lost piece of luggage, the delay, and the bumped seat had put me exactly in the right place for God's timing in both of our lives!

To top it off, a friend spotted me at the hotel as I was attempting to hail a taxi and offered us a ride to church. And a wonderful couple in front of us at church safely returned us to our hotels.

What an adventure! But I knew it had only just begun. I asked if she would like to share dinner, thinking I could be someone to either listen, advise, evangelize, or pray with her—wherever God would lead. We did it all! Although it took a lot of prodding, God finally alerted me to this wonderful opportunity to share him with someone new.

BE AN AMBASSADOR

I am convinced that God's Holy Spirit orchestrates our lives to touch others—strangers, friends, work-related people, service-industry workers, and more—if we would just open up and be ourselves. How? Be free to be in love with Jesus in front of people. Be an ambassador through whom he can introduce himself. There is a world out there hungry and searching for Jesus and his love. Don't keep him to yourself.

Being approachable, inquisitive, and alert is not being pushy. It is not shoving anything down anyone's throat. Instead, these three actions are responsible and manageable responses to initiating conversations with those people God brings along our paths.

Would you reject a friendly, caring individual, especially if you happened to be needy, hurting, lonely, dissatisfied with life—or actually searching for God?

Vicki, my manicurist, didn't. My relationship with her progressed way beyond what I would have ever envisioned. In fact, she was at the top of my prayer list again the next time I kept my hour-long appointment with the King.

FIVE

Follow Up with Care

Become friends, familiar with whom you desire to evangelize; find common interests.
— CHARLES STANLEY

After each nail appointment I had with Vicky my prayer request for her changed. In the beginning I simply added her name to the left-hand side of the page, where I had listed others I was praying for to come to know the Lord. But after each time together, I would begin to pray for specifics such as her happiness, her openness to God, and her inner healing—adding these requests in the space below her name.

As we got to know each other, I found out that her parents died when she was young and that her first marriage had ended a few years earlier. She was dating a nice guy now and was on the verge of getting engaged. Through each conversation, I began to understand her better and better. I asked all kinds of questions that would help me to be both sensitive and caring toward her. As we talked, we really began to like and trust each other, and I always looked forward to seeing her. We were becoming friends.

PREMARITAL COUNSELING

One morning, out of the blue, Vicki asked me, "Do you know a pastor?"

I had to laugh. For all that she knew about me, I guess I had never told her that my youth-worker husband was an ordained minister! So I said, "Actually, Roger is a pastor. Why?"

"Well, my fiancé and I are looking for someone to marry us," she explained.

"Hmmm, well, Rog marries couples, but he requires that they have premarital counseling before he will agree to marry them," I said.

"Oh," she said, "Brandon wouldn't go along with that, I don't think. He's not really into religion."

"I can understand that," I said, "but Rog feels that premarital counseling would be essential before marrying a couple." Trying to sound nonchalant but not haughty, I ended the conversation by saying, "Oh, well, I'm sure you'll be able to work it out."

Thinking that the discussion had been closed, I was taken aback when, at my next appointment, Vicki excitedly said, "Okay!"

I said, "Okay . . . what?"

"Brandon said he would go to one premarital session with Roger!"

I was shocked. Thinking that it was never going to take place, I hadn't thought of all the implications of such an appointment. But now my mind began racing through our similar counseling sessions with other couples, and I was reminded of all the questions my husband would ask about God, church, children ... even sex. I about died on the spot, wishing I hadn't offered my husband as her pastor!

Nevertheless, at the end of my appointment, we arranged a tentative time when they would come over to our house. I left wondering if it would really happen.

But they came the following Tuesday night. Vicki arrived first because she got out of work a bit earlier than Brandon. Feeling a little awkward, I ushered her into the living room. I realized then that I had never seen her in a setting outside of the salon. Like me, she seemed a little uncomfortable. She didn't say much; she just seated herself on the couch and waited quietly for Brandon to arrive.

Our first meeting started off a bit jumbled. Roger had arrived home from work later than usual and was just finishing dinner when Brandon arrived. I felt like a juggler at a circus, trying to make each stranger feel comfortable with the other—including me!

When we all walked into the living room and sat down on two separate couches, the first ten to fifteen minutes went rather smoothly. Rog began to ask them specific questions about their expectations for marriage, and they answered obligingly.

Then we hit a rough spot: God. And everything let loose. The defenses and barriers flew up faster than you could blink your eyes. But it was too late to back out now. We were into it—face to face. It wasn't long before Vicki and I were speechless, shifting our glances back and forth between the two men. The discussion grew more and more heated. Both men hunched forward in their chairs, debating vigorously.

Finally, somehow, the tone of the conversation changed. Brandon said, "I've been waiting since college for someone to convince me there is a God!"

Something—or Someone—had gotten through.

From that moment, all four of us were in a daze. We continued on as if the previous forty minutes had not occurred, and casually finished by scheduling another session before the wedding. *Whew,* I thought, *I'm glad we got through that!*

I was a bit nervous before my next nail appointment with Vicki. I thought she was going to be upset with me for allowing her premarital counseling session to turn into a God debate. I shyly greeted her with a loaded, "How are you?"

She smiled. "I'm really glad we talked through all of those issues the other night."

I was surprised and pleased. I had prepared myself for Brandon to be angry, scared, or confused.

I asked, "So, you and Brandon talked about your beliefs and all?"

She nodded yes without looking up.

I went for it. "Vicki, have you prayed that prayer in the back of my book—kind of like the one we talked about in premarital counseling?"

"Uh-huh," she replied quietly, nodding her head.

I felt more at ease, but I didn't feel like pressing her on the details. I always felt as if Vicki was somewhat fragile. I didn't fully understand why I felt that then, but I knew we would have many more opportunities to talk and share, so we both let the remaining silence change our topic of conversation—for now.

FRIENDS FOR ETERNITY

My prayer list continued to grow for Vicki and now for Brandon, too, as I learned of their needs, hopes, and dreams for the future. Now, as I prayed for Vicki and Brandon, I added to my list: sensitivity to each other, smooth wedding arrangements and, for Brandon, a personal relationship with God.

The wedding day arrived on a warm, sunny summer California day. The wedding was in a beautiful backyard, outdoor setting. Roger and I arrived early enough to meet the groom's family. Brandon's mother greeted us enthusiastically.

"I don't know what you said to my son," she said, "but he's a different person!"

Wow, I thought, *God must have had more in mind when I suggested premarital counseling than I would have ever known!*

The guests were seated near a beautiful pool on the hillside. There we witnessed Vicki and Brandon exchange vows under a white, ivy-covered gazebo.

After the ceremony, we stayed for just a bit, enjoying the sun, flowers, and delicious food. I wanted to share in Vicki's day, but I knew that most of the people from the salon had been her friends much longer, so I stayed in the background. But as we headed for the car, Vicki, dressed in a gorgeous, fitted tea-length gown, ran up to me with open arms.

Filled with the emotion of this event and how it all had unfolded, I hugged her tightly and said, "Vicki, we're going to be friends for life!"

"No," she said, "we're going to be friends for eternity!"

How I wish I had said that! In one sentence it captured so much of what had happened between us. Yes, we were going to be friends here and now—*and* through eternity. Her words told me that she knew the Lord. I was filled with a deep peace and joy.

ALCOHOLICS ANONYMOUS

When Vicki returned from her honeymoon, we looked at pictures and enjoyed the memories of the wedding day. We reminisced over everything—from the chocolate-covered strawberries at the reception to the fun couple they had met while sailing on the Caribbean. And, as usual, I went to her for my manicures.

Then one afternoon she called me at home and asked, "What are you doing tonight?"

I was standing by the stove, eating a carrot. I stopped crunching. This was a rather odd question. We had never done anything social outside of our nail appointments and premarital counseling sessions.

So I asked, a little unsure of myself, "Why, what would you like to do tonight?"

She said, "Would you go with me to an organization for alcoholics?"

"Ummm, sure," I answered, bewildered. I didn't know exactly what to ask or say. She had never given me any prior indication that alcohol was a problem. But I guessed that although Vicki had many, many good friends, she had chosen me to help her because I had been vulnerable with her, and she knew I would not reject her.

"Do you know where a meeting is?" I asked.

She said, "Well, I called and located the one nearest

to my home. Would you want to meet me there at 7:00?"

"Okay," I answered, without any reservation. I wanted her to feel my love and friendship, now more than ever.

I was nervous as I pulled into the unfamiliar parking lot. I had not been to a meeting for alcoholics since 1976, and had just my first (and only) impression to go on, but I felt that tonight Vicki needed an understanding friend who would simply be by her side. And I definitely could understand the fears, the guilt and shame, and especially the out-of-control feelings that can overwhelm a person addicted to alcohol.

We looked for Room 201, stopping at different hallways and doors until we located the stairway up to where we were to meet. At that juncture, we gave each other a quick glance—then not a word till we entered the room.

The lights were dim, candles were lit, and coffee was brewing. Cigarettes were limited to outside of the room, but the faint smell of smoke filtered in. Only after I had been in the room for a few minutes did I realize that this was an all-woman's meeting.

We started with some readings and then the topic was given: Honesty. We were instructed to speak about whatever we wanted to on the subject of honesty during any point in the evening. Without consulting each other, Vicki and I had both decided to be the last to share—if at all!

The first woman spoke of so much personal pain that it felt like a knife opening up an old wound of mine. But there was one difference in our stories: I had found forgiveness. I had hope. She expressed deep hopelessness and then ended her detailed account of personal, ongoing tragedy with, "My name is Anne, and I'm an alcoholic."

I waited for someone to bring words of comfort, a warm hand to her shoulder. No one did.

The next woman shared her fear that she would lose her job as a schoolteacher because of alcohol—for the second time. She was paralyzed with the thought of those consequences but felt unable to help herself. She too ended with her name and confession that she was an alcoholic.

Again, no remarks or words of consolation. I began to get the pattern: Share, then listen silently. I could feel my heart beating faster and faster. My thoughts were running rampant. Every thought from "they need Jesus" to "how will Vicki find help here?" tore at me. Would I just sit here silently? Would I comply with the rules, even though I know the truth that would set them free?

The youngest spoke, a college girl. She was an addict. Trapped. In and out of treatment. She had hit a wall and relapsed. Despair permeated her teary monologue.

Then another young woman spoke through tears as well. She told us she thought she might need to have another abortion, though she had just had one recently.

I was exasperated. How much more pain would I hear tonight without a word about the Savior—who died for us that we might have new life?

Finally it came down to Vicki and me. She said, "My name is Vicki. I think I'm an alcoholic. I'm here because I need help." Done. That was it. No more.

Then I started slowly, afraid of my own adrenalin. "My name is Becky and I'm an alcoholic. I have to tell you, tonight's topic is honesty, and as each of you shared, I've been feeling so much pain. But I need to be honest now. On August 26, 1976, after six years of alcoholism and drug abuse, I met someone who led me to Christ in a simple prayer. And that prayer, where I admitted my sins and asked for God's forgiveness, dramatically changed my life. In fact, God took the desire to drink away from me. Though I can never have a drink and will always be an alcoholic, I know he is the answer for each one of us here. He's the beginning place to look for help."

Then I felt even more boldness come over me, though I was getting both sharp looks from the "elders" and "longing-for-more" looks from the younger women. I finished with, "If Jesus were to walk into this room tonight, he would tell you he loved you. He would put his arms around you. He would help you. Call on him. He is there for you. He is as close as a prayer."

The meeting ended with one more reading. The lights came on, and the college girl quickly came over to me. I had brought along one of my testimony books— just in case—and offered it to her. She took it and looked straight into my eyes and asked, "Will you come back?" I was speechless and sad.

Vicki was ready to leave. As we headed down the steps, I apologized. "Vicki, I'm sorry if I embarrassed you."

"You didn't. Thanks for going with me," she replied.

"Vicki, we need to find you a different meeting. I don't think—"

But before I could finish, Vicki agreed. "This is not the one for me, but I do need help."

A SHORT-HAIRED MENTOR

The next year was filled with both incredible victories and difficult times in Vicki's recovery. She turned to several avenues for healing, including support groups, church, and counseling. My prayer list for Vicki grew to include healing, recovery, understanding, and strength.

Now, over a year later, Vicki is much stronger, happier, and more confident. I love to meet regularly with my friend (and manicurist). I especially love watching her grow more secure and strong in all areas of her life and personality.

Oh, and recently, when I walked into the shop, I couldn't help but notice her hair was cut *short!* In fact, it looked a lot like mine! I blurted out, "Hey, you got your hair cut!"

"Why not?" she replied. "Now I look like my mentor."

I was so taken aback by the choice of her words that I didn't even bring it back up until we had finished our appointment. I leaned over her station and whispered, "Did you mean what you said by calling me your mentor?"

"Yes," she replied quietly.

Vicki was—in her own way—asking me to always follow up on her. So in a recent conversation, I called her just to catch up on life—as friends do—and she confided, "I'm kind of down."

I was immediately concerned, as she had not said this in quite a while, so I asked sincerely, "How can I help?"

She replied, "Just pray for me and tell me you love me."

I did just that, amazed at how honest and vulnerable we had become with each other.

I both know and love Vicki. She's still quiet and shy in many ways. But she's a new person since the first time I met her.

SIX

Know What You Believe

The mission and its message are clear—freedom from the penalty, power, and presence of sin for all who place their trust in Jesus Christ.

—CHARLES STANLEY

When you want to reach people with Christ, begin with the least intimidating approach: prayer. Then ask God—and watch for him—to open up an opportunity for you to share your story with them. Once you have established a relationship of trust and care, you can then share with them the basic facts of Christianity.

Your relationship with God is based not only on faith, but also on facts. Therefore, knowing what you believe, being able to articulate it, and sharing Scripture are crucial to being effective ambassadors of Christ.

I was grateful that my husband "knew his stuff" when he talked with Brandon. Knowledge, when tempered with compassion, provides its own strength and persuasive force.

KEY SCRIPTURES

This point will seem obvious, but I'll make it anyway: In order to share your faith, you've got to know what you believe. Not only that, but you have to be able to communicate your faith in a concise and simple format—a format that you can remember and that your listener can understand. Having these "handles" or key words will keep you from stumbling or drawing a blank—or worse, getting cold feet and never saying anything at all!

One of the classic tools for witnessing is the "Romans Road," four verses from Romans that follow a person's progress from admitting sin to accepting Christ:

For all have sinned and fall short of the glory of God. (Romans 3:23)

But God demonstrates his own love for us in this: While we were still sinners, Christ died for us. (Romans 5:8)

For the wages of sin is death, but the gift of God is eternal life in Christ Jesus our Lord. (Romans 6:23)

If you confess with your mouth, "Jesus is Lord," and believe in your heart that God raised him from the dead, you will be saved. (Romans 10:9)

If you haven't already memorized these verses, I'd encourage you to do so. It's all a part of being effective and confident!

TALKING ABOUT SIN

At the appropriate time, it is important to confront the issue of sin, although it is admittedly uncomfortable for both parties to talk about. Be honest with a nonbeliever that the Bible says the penalty for sin is death. Death, hell, heaven, and eternal life are not easy concepts to agree upon, but they are necessary to discuss.

I have found, especially in America, that the religion of Christianity has been equated with the belief, "If I have been good, or am good enough, I will go to heaven when I die." That incorrect thinking has sent many people, especially young people, away from the church, feeling as if they've blown it so bad already that they cannot be "fixed."

When you share your life with a seeker, acknowledging your own sin is very helpful, because they often can't imagine your life before your conversion. This will help them to identify with you. Tell them the truth; be vulnerable. Even share a struggle you still deal with. Assure them that sin is atoned for by Christ's death on the cross, and we receive a pardon for our sin as a result of accepting his death in our place. Perhaps you could even share how you confessed your sin in a prayer to God, as God himself told us to do (1 John 1:9), then model how it's done.

Last, remind them that Jesus, though sinless, bore our sins. Convey that coming into a relationship with Christ is not just an intellectual exercise; it is a personal encounter. Through faith we accept that a perfect God allowed his Son to endure agony and death on our behalf. This concept often motivates me: being forgiven for so much causes me to love much!

THE LIFE OF JESUS

To know Christ, the seeker will need some understanding of his life here on earth. Usually I have found that I do not have to discuss every historical fact about Jesus with seekers, especially when they are American. However, they need to know some key points.

First, Jesus came into the world through a miracle—the miracle of the virgin birth. Christmastime gives many opportunities for sharing the story of God made man.

Second, knowing about Jesus' death is key to understanding God's sacrifice on our behalf. And his death sets the stage for the greatest miracle of all: his resurrection! This supernatural event conveys the power of God and is one of the main events that makes Christianity unique.

It then becomes exciting and essential to share that Jesus ascended into heaven and lives today. Because he lives, he empowers us with his Holy Spirit so that we may go throughout the world making disciples and baptizing them in his name.

TALKING WITH BOB

My most recent "divine appointment" that challenged if I knew what I believed was on an airplane, with a man named Bob.

We all boarded in a relaxed manner. No rush. No fear of being delayed. There were plenty of empty center seats; therefore, I relaxed into my aisle seat, knowing that the flight would be comfortable.

I unloaded my laptop computer from my carry-on bag so the bag could fit under the seat. I put my "Cadillac" of luggage carts in the overhead compartment and then opened the *InFlight* magazine to pass the time before the welcome and take-off instructions would begin.

As always, I observe. First I glanced to the woman on my right. She had a whole row to herself and soon would be sprawled out, feet stretched, book in hand, nose in book. Vivid printing ... Danielle Steel. *Gee,* I thought, *that author must write a book a month—and everyone reads her!* I've asked many women what they are reading, and they all say, "Danielle Steel." And when I ask why, I get the same response: romance, escape, suspense.

Out of habit, I looked to my left. Oh, a hardback book. A little more intense. So I asked, "What are you reading?"

Stephen King? Okay, I've had it! What do these authors offer to their readers that inspires such loyalty?

Well, the "Steel" woman was way too enthralled in her book to even get into a slight conversation. So, a bit frustrated, I mentioned to the fellow next to me that I write books, too. He looked rather "book-wormish," of slight build and a bit worn from head to toe, but I figured this would stir up a conversation. I knew that I would risk sounding boastful, but my intention and motive was to get into a good conversation about books. As I had calculated, with that comment, we—Bob and I—were off. Off on the subject of books, God, faith, and church. Off on two hours of incredible conversation that seemed predestined.

Bob was not raised to go to church. Now in his forties, he had concluded that there was no God, or at least he had no intention of worrying about it until his death. As he said, "I'll find out then, I suppose." He added, "You can't prove anything about life after death, anyway."

I asked more straight-to-the-point questions of a perfect stranger than I had in a long time. "Have you ever been presented with the Gospel?" I asked boldly, but with genuine interest. An intellectual-type musician, he didn't seem at all angry or frustrated with my line of questions or my subsequent long answers.

For the first hour Bob asked me great lead-in questions. I ended up telling him everything from my testimony to specific incidents detailed in the Bible. But then the newsreel came on.

Aah, I thought, a chance to catch up on the Olympics and other news!

I was just reaching for the earphones when Bob said, "Excuse me, you don't really want to watch the news, do you? You can watch news every day of your life, but we'll never have this conversation again!"

I know my mouth dropped, until I caught it and cleared my throat to cover up my embarrassment. I couldn't believe it! He was interested in talking about having a personal relationship with the living God! Then I realized that people *are* interested in knowing God when he is presented in a relevant, tangible, exciting way.

We continued discussing the idea of making a decision for Christ. I told him about books that validate the historical facts of Christ's death and resurrection, such as *More Than a Carpenter* and *Evidence That Demands a Verdict,* both by Josh McDowell. Finally, however, it was time for the plane to land.

I was getting ready to run off into my own world when Bob said, "Will you pray for me? For these decisions I have to make?"

I handed him my book on prayer and said, "Yes, I'll pray for you, Bob. My address is in the back of my book. Please let me know what you think. You never know, maybe this conversation will lead to an experience with God."

Although I've not heard from Bob yet, I left him with the essentials for coming into a relationship with God, and I've continued to pray for him. One thing I believe: our time was not a waste.

Knowing what you believe should be an integral part of your presentation as an excited evangelist. But don't let *what* you believe take precedence over presenting *who* you know! Remember, the key to effective communication of the Gospel is being able to translate what you believe into memorable, tangible, unforgettable, and appealing "truths" about your personal friend, the Lord Jesus Christ.

SEVEN

Always an Ambassador

We are therefore Christ's ambassadors, as though God were making his appeal through us. We implore you on Christ's behalf: Be reconciled to God.
—2 CORINTHIANS 5:20

Wherever I am, whatever I'm doing, I am being an ambassador for Christ. I learned that lesson in an intense way a few years ago when I embarked on a new project: producing a Christian aerobics video.

Having been an aerobics instructor for almost five years in a large health club, I found that there was very little secular music that I could choose from that didn't either offend a Christian or promote lifestyles and values that I felt were compromising to my faith. That problem finally bothered me enough to do something about it.

I began to daydream with the Lord about putting the best of Christian music to a great workout routine. Finally, I posed the question to the Lord on my prayer list, "Could I make a Christian aerobics video?" It was a rather bold question, especially since only five years earlier I had asked the Lord if I could teach aerobics.

Praying may seem an odd way to prioritize, but when my life is full of family, work, and fun, I've found that the very best way to filter through and prioritize all of my activities is to pray about them, asking God to open and close doors according to his will. After praying, I begin to move in the direction that I believe he is leading.

I prayed about this aerobics project for over one year. Although a few doors opened, nothing really jelled. One morning, however, I was with a publisher friend, and I decided to ask his advice.

"Who would you talk with if you wanted to make a Christian aerobics video?" I asked.

He gave me the name of a person at Benson Music Group and mentioned that this person was, in fact, only a few blocks away. I get real excited at serendipities, when after waiting and looking and watching—at last—a door opens. I ran back to my hotel room, quickly packed, changed, and headed for the convention center where I might find this person . . . and the rest is history.

A GREAT CHOREOGRAPHER

It took almost five months and a lot of prayer to decide to move ahead on an aerobics video. Then, rather late in the process, I suddenly realized that if we really wanted a *great* Christian aerobics video, we needed a *great* choreographer.

That led me on a whole new search, and of course added more requests to my prayer list for the project. Now that I look back, that seems to be the most exciting part of the whole video—praying, searching for, and acquiring the best person we could find to choreograph the video.

Daily I prayed for a great choreographer, sponsors, good music, a shoot sight, apparel, and open doors—then I watched an incredible series of events unfold.

From just mentioning the project to a new acquaintance, I was given the name of Candice Copeland-Brooks, a recent Fitness Instructor of the Year and an international presenter (someone who leads an aerobics class). She was also well-known in the fitness industry and was a national Step Reebok trainer. Once I got her name, I needed a phone number. So, from an airport, I telephoned a woman who knew Candice—a woman who, in fact, was going out of town that day for the next three weeks. She told me about Candice's reputation in the fitness industry and if I could get her, I'd—you guessed it—have the best!

Within that week, I received an application to attend a workshop that Candice Copeland-Brooks would be presenting for Reebok, only twenty miles from my home! I had never attended a fitness workshop before and wasn't sure how I would meet Candice, but I was sure that I would at least introduce myself to her.

Upon entering the mirrored workout room, I saw over fifty fit aerobic instructors and wasn't sure how I would recognize Candice. Then in the corner of the room, I spotted a petite, muscular, fair-skinned instructor who was eight months pregnant. Her black bike shorts and lacy leotard set off her pony-tailed, light blonde hair. Without a doubt, this was Candice Copeland-Brooks.

I was so nervous. But when I saw a chance to slip to the front of the room and introduce myself, I blurted out everything at once: "Hi, my name is Becky Tirabassi. Your friend suggested that I contact you about choreographing an aerobics video. Would you be interested in choreographing a Christian aerobics video?"

"Umm," she replied matter-of-factly, "just give my office a call."

I was a wreck. I thought I had blown it. But, in fact, I found out later that she called our mutual friend and told her that I had approached her about the video— and wondered why I made it so definite that I was doing a *Christian* aerobics video. What did I think she was, an atheist?

Even though I was afraid Candice would turn me down, I called her office that next week and we chatted. I sensed immediately that her background, expertise, and experience were beyond what I would have ever dreamed of having for our project—and so was her normal fee. But amazingly—and she even wondered why herself—she cut her fee in half and we were able to move forward—together!

From that day on, Candice went to the top of my prayer list. I prayed for our professional relationship, her spiritual life, and the success of our project. As I got to know her, each time we would talk a little more about subjects other than aerobics. After rehearsal segments while resting on a step, or when taking a hydration break, she would reveal bits of her past, such as being a dancer and actress in high school and college, and then how she developed as a leading trainer in the fitness industry over the past ten years. I was always so impressed, as if I was truly with a star.

From her comments, I began to understand more clearly how she felt about God. For instance, our dialogue about the music selection cued me in to her sensitivity to pushy religionists. Other times we would take a short break and she would share about her upbringing in a mainline, liturgical church, similar to my background. With just a few leading questions, I found out that Candice, like most of us in our twenties, grew disillusioned with such a stoic church setting and quit going to church. I surmised from our similar religious backgrounds that she believed there was a God, but having a personal relationship with the living God was the missing link. In fact, a few times I even heard her—in passing—mention her own spiritual search.

I kept these little spiritual details to myself, but stored them away for a time when we could discuss them, not as facts, but as something more. For now, work—or working out—was our chief purpose in meeting. One day I hoped, though, that a friendship might follow, even if our lives and professions seemed worlds apart.

Each time before Candice and I met, I asked the Lord to provide an opportunity for me to talk a little about him. In fact, before one meeting, I asked the Lord if perhaps Candice could bring up God, instead of my always being the initiator of that subject. And should I have been surprised when she decided on that very rehearsal day to share about her spiritual search and journey of the past few years? As she detailed her trip to the Himalayas and her trek to the peaks of huge mountains in search for inner peace, I stood there with my mouth shut, quietly listening, but inside I was doing cartwheels, knowing that I had prayed specifically that day that she would bring up her thoughts on God.

Among our many challenges was having to pick out

all of the Christian music together. I especially wanted her perspective of what would be cutting-edge music that would meet industry standards for aerobics. I hoped that my desires for Christian music would fit her standards. To my amazement, we agreed on lyrics, beat, and the placement of each song—every time!

Other details fell into place as well. The process of solving all the Christian production dilemmas—such as working with secular contributors, getting the licenses to use the music, and choosing moderate apparel and dance moves—gave Candice many opportunities to see how God was involved in creating this video.

I decided not to hold back on my natural way of talking out loud to the Lord about what I'm thinking. Often I would tell her how I felt the Lord had "opened doors," or how he seemed to have orchestrated all the details of this project, bringing together Reebok, The Sports Step Company, and the music of Benson Music Group. The dream was coming true in front of our eyes!

SHOOTING THE VIDEO

The video project was greater and more exciting than I could have ever imagined. My prayer list for the video grew from one line to two pages. I prayed and placed into God's care all the little steps and decisions that had to be taken before the project was finished, everything from finding the perfect shoes and apparel to learning the aerobics routine to my friendship with Candice.

And then the time came to shoot the video.

I flew to Nashville, and once there, I was pretty much a wreck. Have you ever gotten yourself into a project so deep, then wondered if you are even capable of pulling it off? One thing I knew for sure, without Candice, I couldn't do it!

On the first day of rehearsals, I picked up my two friends who were going to be in the video with me, and we headed over to a rehearsal studio with Candice and our producer, Joseph. It was a rather odd evening— after the rehearsal, we all went to dinner and then to a laundromat! (Four sets of sweaty workout clothes were more than our hotel rooms could handle for the next few days.)

But once again, as we rehearsed the step moves on the curbside, ate tacos, and folded clothes, we also talked about our individual relationships with the Lord.

The next day's rehearsal was much more grueling physically and emotionally, but at the end of it, we had this overwhelming feeling that God was really giving us the energy and excitement we needed to complete this project. In fact, at various times, we would pray for little glitches to work out: we prayed that a broken air conditioner would work again and that Candice's baby would be comfortable with his hotel baby-sitter. Pieces seemed constantly to fall together—with the ultimate hope and prayer that we would perform at our very best.

It seemed a pleasant and welcomed advantage that we were able to call on God at any moment, for any reason—and it never seemed awkward or out of place. Though I never wanted to offend Candice because of her professionalism and her high profile in the fitness industry, neither did I want to ignore or compromise my spontaneity in talking to or calling upon God to help us. And I never had to!

On the day of the shoot, Candice reminded me that

I must take off all of my jewelry. I asked her if she would wear my cross for me so I wouldn't have to leave it in my hotel room. She surprised me when she said, "I've often admired your cross. I once had a confirmation cross, but lost it quite a few years ago. I would love to wear it!"

As the day rolled on and technical and lighting difficulties played their unwritten parts in the script, we would often stop and pray.

Near the close of the shoot, Adam—Candice's nursing baby—was overcome by the Nashville heat, the noisy crew, and the fact that he couldn't be in his mom's arms at that very moment. Even though he had seen his mom during a set-change break, Adam began to howl just as the music started. I could see on Candice's face the anguish of being torn between her role as mother and her job as choreographer.

I asked the director and camera crew if we could take just a moment to pray for Adam. So, right on the floor, where we were positioned for leg lifts, we began to pray. As we prayed we heard Adam crying loudly through the closed double doors. We prayed out loud for Adam to be comforted for the few short hours left. Within minutes he stopped crying!

In the early part of the day we prayed individually, but at the end of the day, we—cast, crew, producers, director, and choreographer—held hands in a circle and prayed together. With great excitement I watched Candice that day, seeing her growing openness to and awareness of God.

Something else occurred that day for me, though. From the start I knew that I would need Candice on the set to cue and encourage me, but I didn't realize just how nervous and dependent I would be upon her for every little move in the choreography. I must have rehearsed so hard that I was blanking out for whole portions of the routine. My only option was to completely rely on Candice by lip-reading and mimicking her every move. And so I did. In the beginning, it was hard to let go of my own intuition and put my trust in her for everything, but I had no other recourse if we were to film full twenty-minute segments in one shot.

We would start each segment with her countdown, and as soon as the music and film began to roll, I would be glued to her lips. I would speak only when she did, and if I would get overly confident, I usually miscounted. So I learned early on to "stick by the teacher." She would direct me to the left or right with a point of a finger and would often nod and smile upon seeing my eyes respond and my body perform correctly. Besides being somehow funny, responding to her directions was a magnetic feeling. I lifted my knees or pressed my hands down simply by following the silent command of my human mirror.

By midnight, when we had completed the entire video shoot, I said, "I've never done so much lip-reading in one day."

Candice replied, "I've never had anyone lip-read as well as you!"

We laughed, but something had happened between us as a result of all that eye contact and proven trust. After just a moment's reflection, I said, "You know, we've become soul mates!"

A LITTLE GOLD CROSS

Candice and I returned to Los Angeles. The following week, we made an appointment to have lunch together. More than anything, I wanted to express my gratitude and respect for her with a gift. I decided on a cross—a beautiful gold cross—and even if she never wore it, it would be a token of my love and friendship.

Candice's husband joined us for lunch, and that made me a little more embarrassed, but I still handed her the wrapped box shortly after she sat down. As she opened it, I couldn't tell how she really felt about it, but she did comment that it was pretty. Later that month, she dropped me a note to tell me she hadn't taken it off since the day I gave it to her!

A few more months passed and my new friend had an incredibly busy, international schedule that proceeded to sap her strength and completely wear her out. Our first conversation after her month away was filled with updating each other with facts. I had anticipated a call to come shortly after her trip, but when it came in the evening instead of during working hours, I retreated to the laundry room for quiet and privacy. I hoisted myself up onto the washing machine and poked my head out the back screen door to view the evening stars. We chatted for the next hour about babies, travel, events, the video, and more.

We both seemed genuinely interested in the progress of each other's projects or any fun news of each other's children and spouses. But somehow I didn't pick up on what she was feeling.

A day later, she called again. This time she told me that she had been really searching for "something," and in her search she had picked up my book, *Let Prayer Change Your Life,* which I had sent to her even before we officially began the *Step into Fitness* video. She had just finished reading the book from cover to cover. I was holding my breath with sheer excitement, uncertain but anticipating what she was going to tell me. She simply relayed that through the chapters she had found her answers—and had prayed the words of the closing prayer in the back of the book. We had become "soul mates" for eternity!

After she finished telling me of her experience, I literally cried. I said, laughing through my tears, "I'm so happy for you."

"I knew you would be!" she said, laughing in reply.

When she appeared on *The Home Show* for an aerobic demonstration just a few weeks after her "prayer," the camera zoomed in on her, and all I could see was a little gold cross hanging from her neck.

Now Candice and I share a mutual "coaching" relationship: She coaches me physically, and I coach her spiritually!

EIGHT

The Power of Prayer

In regard to my own experience, I will say that unless I had the spirit of prayer, I could do nothing. If I lost the spirit of grace and supplication, even for a day or an hour, I found myself unable to preach without power and efficiency, or to win souls by personal conversation.
—CHARLES FINNEY

In all the opportunities I have had to speak of my faith—with Vicki, Brandon, Candice, Sylvia, and various travel acquaintances—prayer has been my strongest asset. Purposeful, daily, diligent, persevering prayer has enabled me to reach out to everyone around me, from acquaintances to loved ones, with the good news of salvation. Prayer is not the only resource for evangelism that I have or actively use, but it is a crucial—indeed, non-negotiable—part of my evangelism strategy.

It was Leonard Ravenhill's powerful writing on prayer and revival that challenged me. He said, "Let the record stand. The men who prayed the most, accomplished most!" This does not mean that we should become great producers of fruit for our own sake or reputation. But we do need to communicate continually with God for his direction for our lives, with our goal being to accomplish much for his kingdom.

Prayer opens us to God's nudges of opportunity, especially when we meet new people. In Candice's case, I knew that she could not have cared less that I was in ministry or was a believer who prayed for her. What mattered to her was that I cared for her and shared my life with all its problems, pains, and joys.

Early in my relationship with Candice, I felt more spiritually sensitive than our friendship was ready for. At that time prayer served a great purpose. First, it became my avenue for lifting Candice up to the Lord, creating within me an anticipation that God would and could do the impossible. Through prayer I began to believe that power for change would be released. Second, prayer enabled me to grow in concern and love for her. Third, my prayer list kept me focused on her specific needs and on opportunities to introduce her to the Lord.

Let's explore these three points a bit further.

Prayer is an avenue for lifting someone up to the Lord.

Hudson Taylor, before leaving England for China to spearhead what would become an incredible evangelism explosion on that continent, said, "Move man, through God, by prayer alone!"

How can you and I practically, in the nineties, "Move man, through God, by prayer alone?" The most effective way that I have found to see others come to Christ, especially those who don't live near me, is to make—and maintain—a prayer request list. On that list

I include family, friends, and co-workers. Over the years I have seen many people on that list convert to Christ. At the same time, I have become convinced that my prayers can and do make a difference!

Praying for people to come to know the Lord is not my way of getting everyone to be like me. I'm not trying to get people to become an evangelist, or even to believe everything exactly as I believe. Instead, I pray that they will not run from Jesus. I pray that they will be freed of their misconceptions of him. And most of all, I pray that people will experience the love of Jesus and really come to know the person of Jesus Christ.

I'm convinced that it is my prayer list that forces me to act upon my good intentions! It is a visual reminder, prodding and encouraging me to evangelize.

For instance, today the first page of my request list looks like this:

> Lord, teach me to be a . . .
> bold evangelist
> sincere communicator
> friendly neighbor
> kind customer
> concerned stranger
> good friend
> fair employer
> loyal employee

As Leonard Ravenhill said, "Prayer goes far beyond using God as a means of escape or relief. It is seeking a love for the will of God among men, for the manifestation of the power of God among men, and for the recovery of the glory of God among men."

I've discovered that good evangelism does not

require great theological knowledge. But evangelism definitely does require prayer. People are not "skins" to be caught. They are searching for answers, and I have the answer. I do not need to be shy or afraid; instead, I need to be determined to be prayerful.

Prayer helps you develop love and concern for the person you are praying for.

When my prayer list grows in specifics for someone—for her happiness, her healing, or her future—I genuinely begin to care about the outcome of these requests. For example, I would call Vicki when I thought of her. I asked her questions and gave her cards or books to encourage her. As a result, I began to love her.

Steve is another person who made it onto my prayer list. I used to lead a Campus Life group, and he was the brother of one of the members. Steve had struggled with alcohol since high school. Like me, he had used alcohol as a tool for partying; he had never meant it to turn into an addiction. But it had. And once you're addicted, the way out is almost always tough.

One day Steve called to see if he could come over and talk to me. He told me that he was leaving the next day to enlist in the Navy. I wasn't sure, but I had an idea of what he wanted to talk about. It's funny how you can know someone for a few years and never really get down to the nitty gritty, but when someone is leaving, somehow they are more willing to bare their soul. And that's what happened.

Steve knew my story of how I had become an alcoholic, and we had talked a few times over the last two years. So when we sat down on my couch to talk, I wasn't surprised when Steve told me he thought he might have a drinking problem. He was genuinely concerned about what would happen to him during his tour with the Navy. We talked openly of the possibilities, and then we prayed and asked God to help him.

When Steve left that night, he went to the top of my prayer list. For three years, I prayed that he would know God and be healed from the desire to drink. Sometimes he would write me a brief letter, or I would hear about him through his family. But nothing significant happened.

One day I was on a television show out East. I was asked to share my story of alcoholism and then asked to pray for anyone who might be watching who needed God and needed release from an addiction to alcohol. During the prayer, I became unusually emotional, even choking up with tears. That seemed odd, because I hadn't been very emotional at all during the entire interview. But when I offered the prayer, I said, "If you would just like to get on your knees and ask God to heal you and to come into your life, please pray this prayer with me . . ."

When I arrived home the following day, I went into my office and pushed the button to my answering machine. Steve's voice was on the machine!

"Becky," he said, "this is Steve. I came in this weekend from a huge binge. I turned the television on, flicked through a few stations, and there you were. I knelt down and prayed that prayer with you. I haven't told you, but I'm stationed in California. What are you doing this weekend? Please call me back."

Unbelievable. Not only had God enabled me to pray for Steve daily for three years, but he had given me an opportunity to witness to him from three thousand miles away—without even knowing it! And best of all, Steve had responded! For me, this is the proof of the power of prayer.

Steve's story has a great ending. Though his recovery was difficult, and not without a few setbacks, Steve has found his niche helping others in similar situations by becoming a rehabilitation counselor for the Navy. Not only that, but Steve is actively growing in his relationship with the Lord. In fact, I wouldn't be surprised to see him in ministry some day.

Then there was Jeff. He was a handsome young high-school wrestler who found every reason to party, until he came to our Campus Life group, where he heard and accepted the love of Jesus. Like many other Campus Life kids, he graduated from high school and went on to college, but I continued to pray for him. I prayed that he would read the Bible, go to church, join a campus Christian organization, and really get to know and love God. Praying for him and other kids I had discipled seemed a great opportunity to affect their lives now that they were miles away. Besides, if they were half of what I was like in college, I needed to be very faithful in my prayers for them!

And as the pattern goes, the longer my Campus Life members were away at school, the further away from God they seemed to grow—and Jeff was no exception! We would see each other occasionally, when he would return for the summers or holidays, but distance grew in our relationship, as it had between him and God. I would often say, "I'm praying for you," and he would give me that funny smile that said, "I wish you weren't!"

Then one evening, after we had moved to California, I got a phone call. "Becky, this is Jeff. I wanted you to be the first to know. For one year, a fraternity brother of mine has been bugging me to go to a campus Bible study. Well, I went last night and dedicated my life to the Lord."

I was stunned. Exactly how I had been praying for Jeff almost five years: Go to a Bible study and dedicate his life to the Lord. Wow!

His last request on the phone that night was, "Will you pray for me?"

"Jeff," I replied, "I *have* been praying for you!"

Now Jeff's requests on my prayer list grew and changed. I prayed, "Help him to grow, Lord; give him strength in these beginning days as a committed Christian in a college setting."

I got a few calls from Jeff over the next few months, asking for prayer for friends and family members. Then one day, just as unexpectedly as his first, I received another call.

"Becky." It was Jeff. "I believe God is calling me into full-time ministry with high-school kids! Will you pray for me?" There was a brief, awkward pause. Then he said, "Uhh, will you also consider financially supporting me?"

How great! After all those prayers, not only has a former Campus Life member really solidified his walk with the Lord, but now he's going into full-time ministry!

"Of course I will support you," I exclaimed. So I have, through my prayers *and* my money. And it has been great to watch him—and his ministry—grow and grow and grow!

I grew to love Steve and Jeff because I prayed for them. When you begin to pray for people who are struggling, your prayers for them increase your concern for their physical, emotional, and spiritual welfare.

Prayer reminds us to stay alert and aware of evangelistic opportunities.

My research and experience alike have proven to me that without purposeful, diligent time spent with God, we will not have the purity or the passion necessary for spontaneous, enthusiastic, bold evangelism.

Therefore with great anticipation, I look for opportunities to be the person I've asked God to make me. And when I pray, I am in awe to see how God leads me.

Praying for Candice to become a Christian made all the difference in my efforts to share my faith with her. It increased my willingness to share my story at each meeting and kept me deliberate and focused in my conversations with her about God. In addition, my prayers for her made me alert to any open doors or opportunities as they occurred.

That's how Candice and I became soul mates. When we have prepared with prayer, we will be alert to the opportunities for evangelism God brings into our lives. Simply spoken, because of all the unusual and unexplainable answers to prayer I have seen and received, I now *expect* God to answer our prayers!

NINE

Praying People into the Kingdom

The most powerful activity you can participate in is prayer. That is why you need to think through what you are praying for another individual. Nothing so moves the circumstances of life as prayer does.
—CHARLES STANLEY

When we are looking for people to pray into the kingdom, we often overlook the obvious: our very own neighbors!

At the same convention where I committed myself to pray for one hour a day, a former president of Youth for Christ, Kelly Beihl, shared how he prayed daily for his neighbors to become Christians. I remember being very impressed and convicted by the thought of a college president who made time to pray for his neighbors. I began to pray for my neighbors too. But it took over two years for me to put those prayers into action.

PRAYING FOR MY NEIGHBORS

The first eight years of my marriage, we lived near my family and worked at my alma mater. Then, in a whirlwind of exciting circumstances, Roger, Jake, and I moved from Cleveland, Ohio to southern California. Everything seemed to fall into place—everything, that is, except for the most crucial detail: a home to live in.

Over the summer we stayed in the home of a church member until we could find a location and home that was just right for us. But it seemed that anything that was "just right" was also out of our budget!

With one week left to buy a home, clear escrow, and be out of the rental house before the church family returned, we walked into a storefront, family-owned real estate office and shared our woes with a stranger—who turned out to be a fellow Christian.

Within the week, my husband and the realtor had narrowed our choices down to three. The first house they showed me had that "feeling" that only a woman gets. You know the one: "This is our house! I could call this home . . ."

That afternoon, we put a bid in on the house and it was accepted. Within thirty days we moved in to become the neighbors of Barbara on one side and Jean on the other.

So one of my first duties upon moving into our new home and neighborhood was to find out the names of my neighbors and to pray for them.

And I did! From the time I learned my neighbors' names I placed them on the left side of my prayer list, under *salvation,* and for three and a half years I prayed for them to come to know the Lord and to know his love—that is, until I heard Charles Stanley on the radio one morning.

It was the week of Easter. As usual, on Mondays, Wednesdays, and Fridays I taught aerobics. On my way home, I would always turn the radio to "In Touch," Charles Stanley's daily show. This particular morning he was talking about prayer. With my convertible top down and radio blaring (even my husband has occasionally accused me of trying to evangelize the streets simply by driving around and letting my radio preach the message), I caught my morning inspiration.

Then it happened. Dr. Stanley said one of those sentences that a preacher says nice and slow, so that you not only hear it, but can't forget it.

He said simply, "Don't pray about anything you wouldn't want God to do through you!"

For the past three years, I had been daily and diligently praying for my neighbors to become Christians, thinking that surely God would have someone in their families or workplaces offer to take them to church or nonchalantly share Christ with them—and that my prayers would be a part of that! But this was the first time I realized that the one who would share with them might be *me*.

I had often considered sharing my faith with one neighbor, Barbara, because we were about the same age and had children that played together regularly. But, I rationalized, getting into the whole spiritual thing, sharing with Barbara, a busy, single mom, might hinder our neighborly, surface relationship.

The instant Dr. Stanley said those words, I felt that they were for *me*, words not only to convict me, but also for me to *act* upon. And God, I'm sure, timely in setting up little divine appointments, didn't give me a whole lot of room to forget or shrug this concept off.

CHURCH ON SUNDAY

On Good Friday, Barbara unexpectedly showed up on my doorstep, offering to chip in a few dollars for a pizza our children had shared the night before. As always, Barbara was perfectly dressed in her size-five shorts. Her blonde bob and manicured nails were flawlessly in place—whether for work or recreation. She had that eternal "California girl" look. And being a single mom for the past few years had really kept her moving at a fast pace.

Without any premeditation (except for a good dose of healthy conviction that had prodded me earlier in the week), out of my mouth came the words, "Barbara, I just want you to know that I pray for you every day." Thud. The words came out so loud and clear and strong that both of us were in shock. Tears immediately sprang to our eyes.

Obviously, this comment had without warning taken our relationship from the surface to something just a bit deeper. Feeling the awkwardness of the silence, I asked, "Would you like to go to church with us this Sunday?"

Easter Sunday was one of the most inspirational and evangelistic services that our church had, and I knew from previous conversations with Barbara that she liked to read the books that my pastor had written.

Still stunned and groping for words, Barbara said, "Well, thank you, but I would hate to go to church just once a year. I think I would feel guilty."

I knew I was heading into foreign territory, but since I was in this deep I went on. So I replied gently but with a little laugh, "I'd hate to think guilt would keep you out of church!"

She said, "You know, it's very thoughtful for you to invite us, Becky, but we have a lot of relatives to visit with and—"

I could tell in her voice that she was searching for reasons to decline, so I quickly interrupted. "I understand, but any time that would be good for you would work out for us, because we have seven services on Easter Sunday!"

I knew immediately that my ability to accommodate her was just about the last straw! She was looking a little frustrated when my son ran up behind her on the way into the house, with a train of children following behind him. "Mom," he suggested very matter-of-factly, as if he had been listening to the whole conversation, "why don't you just invite Barbara inside to talk?"

What a novel idea—Barbara had never been in my house! In all these years, she had come over looking for kids, but had never sat down inside or even seen the rooms of my home.

"Barbara, would you like to come in?" I invited.

As the next few hours unfolded, I listened to and shared with my neighbor. I found out for the first time why she was a single mom. We talked about her mother's death, which had just taken place a few years earlier. I inquired of her religious upbringing. We even talked about her future dreams and plans. Then I showed her my prayer notebook, and I explained why and how I prayed for her, actually showing her the page her name was on.

It turned out to be a friendly, relaxing time of discovery and disclosure. Sensing her appreciation, but knowing she wasn't sure what to say, I offered to pray. Because of a near-panicked look in her eye, I bowed my head quickly before she could decline and briefly thanked the Lord for our time together and for our friendship.

When we both looked up, each seated on a living room couch, I offered one more time, "Would you like to go to church with us on Sunday?"

Barbara sweetly, but firmly said, "I really don't know, Becky." So, thinking fast, I suggested that she leave a message on my answering machine on Saturday if she would like to go. She left then, but not before I had loaded her down with an armful of tapes, a few books, and even a prayer notebook.

Saturday came—and went. No answering machine messages about church. And I knew that I had said enough and offered enough times that much more might become offensive. So Saturday evening I set my alarm to allow enough time for my son and I to get ready for the 11:00 A.M. service, where we planned to meet with my husband, the college pastor, and sit together.

EASTER SUNDAY

At 8:00 A.M. the telephone rang in my ear.

"Hello," I whispered groggily.

"Becky?" It was Barbara. "The kids and I were wondering if you might be going to the 9:00 A.M. service. Would it be okay if we joined you?"

My mind raced. There was every reason why the 9:00 A.M. service was not going to work: (1) there was not enough time to get ready (only about 20 minutes—and I was still in bed), (2) it would be the most crowded due to visitors, (3) and the parking would be the most congested. But out of my mouth came the words, "Sure, we'll pick you up in about twenty minutes."

The race was on! I flew into my son's bedroom, lifted him out of bed and onto his feet, and frantically announced, "We're going to church—*now!* Get dressed!" Then I proceeded to get ready for church in the shortest amount of time ever recorded for an Easter Sunday.

I was still putting on earrings and mascara as we headed out the door to pick up our next-door neighbors, and Jake was still buttoning his shirt. But we were so excited! Our neighbors were going to church with us!

We drove as quickly as possible to church, then parked in the street about a block away. We ran through the crosswalk, pushed into the church, and dashed up to an usher.

He shook his head regretfully. "No more seats," he said.

I felt like crying. I wanted so badly for Barbara's first visit to church to be just perfect. Frustrated, but not ready to give up yet, my eyes searched the rows and balconies for a place for us to sit. Then I spotted five seats at the top of the west balcony! But we were still in the narthex, in the center of the church.

I looked at our little troop and determinedly whispered, "Follow me." We charged up the steps and through the church. Amazingly, we reached our destination just in time to be seated, then immediately stood for the "Hallelujah Chorus." It was breathtaking—and I was out of breath!

The service seemed ideally planned for the person I

had brought. After singing anthems we both knew from childhood and hearing a moving testimony, the sermon unfolded: "Life's not fair, but God is good." Each illustration and Scripture seemed designed to comfort a person in my neighbor's situation. But my greatest satisfaction came when, with tears in her eyes, she looked at me over three little heads and whispered, "I was supposed to be here!"

What a special day it was! Before we had even returned to our van, she invited us all over to her house for a barbecue. Later in the week we took the kids on a long bike ride, where we continued our talks about church, God, and faith.

ONE LOST SHEEP

When Saturday arrived, I remember thinking, "Well, let's not push things, especially since our head pastor will be out of town." I decided I would wait a few weeks before inviting her to church again.

But just as I was walking in the front door that afternoon, the phone rang. It was Barbara.

"Becky," she said, "the kids are gone this weekend, but I wondered if I could go to church with you tomorrow?"

I was speechless. I didn't even have to ask her! Incredibly, I began to backpedal, saying, "Our pastor won't be there this week. Are you sure you want to go?"

Without hesitation she answered, "Yes. Sure. That will be another experience!"

Surprised and a bit ashamed by her ready response, I wished that I had said that—and with as much confidence as she had. So we went ahead and made plans for the following morning.

Wouldn't you know it? The guest pastor spoke on Matthew 18:12–14, about the shepherd who has one hundred sheep. When one strays, he leaves the ninety-nine and goes out to find the one lost sheep. Again, we both knew that Barbara was supposed to be there!

Those two Sundays began a whole new level of friendship for Barbara and me. Now when we see each other, we share our thoughts about God, prayer, or our futures. Occasionally we attend church together or share lunches, and often we stop to chat amidst armloads of groceries or laundry.

Because God had finally nudged me into sharing him with Barbara, I had gained not only a fellow believer—but a good friend as well.

TEN

Common Mistakes and Mixed Messages

Preach the Word; be prepared in season and out of season; correct, rebuke and encourage—with great patience and careful instruction.
— 2 TIMOTHY 4:2

We've already talked about the importance of looking for a hook to engage someone in conversation, and the importance of knowing what we believe in order to communicate it clearly. But we also need to avoid some common mistakes and mixed messages that keep us from effectively sharing our faith.

As you read along, ask yourself if you have indulged in any of these mistakes or mixed messages. If you can eliminate any of them, your effectiveness in evangelism will increase greatly!

Mistake #1: Trying to "close the sale"
the first day you meet someone.

It is important for all Christians to understand that there is more than one style of evangelism. Mass evangelism, whether at a crusade, rally, or outreach event, is one form of evangelism. Spirit-led boldness is another form of evangelism that takes place with individuals or in small groups. Its persistence should be determined by (1) the Spirit's prompting, (2) the length of time you have together, and (3) the degree of privacy and comfortableness you have with each other.

With Vicki, my nail technician, I knew that I had regular opportunities to meet her one-on-one. I was allowed the luxury of time, so I could progress slowly. With Candice, my choreographer, the amount of time we had together was six months, so I came to each session more prepared with questions and discussion starters, rather than just waiting for an opportunity to arise over time. But when time is limited, as on an airplane, bus, or in a grocery line, God still can provide open doors for impromptu, Spirit-led opportunities for sharing one's faith. One rule of thumb might be to gauge the boldness of your conversation by the amount of time you will have together.

Mistake #2: Putting down someone's religious background the first time you meet.

When you meet someone from another religious background, you should not immediately attack them for their beliefs. This mistake can close doors faster than anything! Again, you must first consider the length of time that you have with a person when you weigh out the route you should take.

First of all, ask a lot of questions about an unfamiliar religion or cult. Don't assume you know all the facts about what they believe unless you've had first-hand experience or have had occasion to study what they believe.

Once they articulate what it is they believe, you should be able to identify some of your major differences. At that juncture, when you have the opportunity, you can articulate what you believe and how your beliefs are different. You do not need to prove they are wrong and you are right, but it is fair to reveal where and why you differ.

A friend of mine had this occur within his family circle. Initially both parties chose to discuss the differences in detail and defend their own positions by letter, sharing references and resources. Then there came a time of non-negotiation and even of awkward silence. At that point the two relatives made a mutual decision to close the debate for the time being. The person involved in the alternative religion felt attacked, and the Christian, who had intellectually argued a Christian's set of beliefs, felt that he was rejected on those points. Therefore, in order to remain as cordial friends—and family members—it was best to put the subject to rest. This allowed both parties to be fully aware of the other's beliefs, if either ever wanted to approach them again, but it also allowed the families to function congenially—with an open-door policy for the future, rather than a completely shut door.

Mistake #3: Assuming or pre-judging another's relationship with God.

You can never truly know all the aspects of what another truly feels or believes, but you can get some good indicators and clues by asking the right questions.

Whenever I talk with folks, I almost always share my testimony or story. It serves to break down any barriers that I am—or was—always a "good" Christian, and it clearly paints the picture that I had a great need for salvation. It details how I was saved and shows that I actually received a new life. I try to include that I became "a brand-new person" as a result of my relationship with Jesus. I think this is unique to Christianity and offers seekers a great deal of hope.

By being vulnerable and divulging my sins and shortcomings I eliminate a lot of denominational misconceptions and questions that people often have about God. It also puts our conversation about him on a relational track, rather than a religious track. Often a story will increase a listener's curiosity, and they'll ask questions. But if they continue to remain shy—or stunned!—I'll ask them a few questions, such as:

- Did you ever go to church? What kind (or denomination)?

By asking this question, I can get a picture of what they learned or believed as children and how these impressions may influence what they believe now. In addition, asking about their past is usually less threatening and less nosey than, "Do you go to church?" That is a good question, but it can often come later.

- What is your occupation?

The type of job they have and what their hobbies and priorities are can also give you an idea of what they consider important. In return, they will often ask about your occupation or hobbies, and then you are able to move the conversation in a direction you are comfortable with.

Once I gather up as much information as I can, I almost see myself as a troubleshooter. Wherever their weakest link is to God, that is where I begin to present biblical ideas to their comments, sandwiching them between real-life stories and experiences.

Assuming is usually premature. Asking questions and listening carefully provides a much clearer picture—more quickly!

If the mistakes haven't tripped you up yet, beware of the mixed messages that we can give people!

Mixed Message #1: You need to go to my church.

One of the churches we have attended in our fifteen years of marriage had a very high profile in our community and a very large Sunday morning attendance. One couple I invited to our church felt very uncomfortable about coming with us, for a number of reasons. For one thing, they wanted to locate a church closer to their home. I encouraged them to do so, and within just a few weeks they were regular attenders! Before long, their pastor had visited them in their home and had invited them to a Sunday school class. Before the year was up, one of my new friends had even been baptized and confirmed.

There are many aspects involved in choosing a church, including one's previous religious experience, the quality of the youth or Sunday school program, the location, and the preaching style of the pastor—just to list a few.

You might as well face it—it is possible that not everyone you invite to church will be comfortable with *your* church! Always be open to suggesting other solid, Christian, "alive" churches in their vicinity in order to help them find the church that is the very best for them.

Don't take it personally, and don't be a judge. Be a facilitator.

Mixed Message #2: You don't have to go to church to be a Christian.

Going to church is for growth, fellowship, learning, and accountability. A church home is where you give financially, spiritually, and physically of your gifts and talents to build up the body of Christ on earth. When a Christian procrastinates in finding or attending a local church body, they are both hurting themselves and hindering their observers.

To continually or seasonally eliminate church attendance for work or hobby or sleep is to cut off your own supply of fuel, food, and fire—and it models a laziness after God to those around you who might be seeking.

The New Testament exhorts believers not to forsake gathering together with fellow believers. Because American Christians are busy and hardworking, many denominations are offering services during the week, on Saturday evening, and several times on Sunday in order to accommodate many different lifestyles. Find a time and service that suits you.

Finally, if you are embroiled in church problems, seek to reconcile the problem or move on; don't use the problems as an excuse to quit attending church.

Mixed Message #3: I can live any way I want and be a Christian.

It is ridiculous to think that our actions are not speaking louder than our words when others are observing our Christianity. Foul language, lying, drunkenness, cheating, and gossiping are not fruits of the

Christian life. To continually or regularly partake in the above list—or the more silent weapons, such as jealousy, lust, or bitterness—and tell others you are a Christian does an injustice to the world and to other Christians who have to follow behind you.

One of my saddest experiences is to tell strangers that I am a Christian and have them equate my faith to that of fallen television evangelists. They are repulsed by my beliefs, even before I get a chance to defend them. It is not just for our own witness that we need to "be above reproach," but for the sake of others representing the gospel, as well.

Not that we will be perfect, but even admissions of wrongdoing and apologies for our behavior go a long way with nonbelieving neighbors or co-workers. Even if we are struggling with a difficult sin, it is better to be honest with others to the degree that is appropriate and be willing to seek professional help, if necessary, than to pretend the problem doesn't exist.

Credibility, integrity, consistency, and humility will have a powerful impact on every facet of your daily life as an evangelist. You might even be surprised that, without even mentioning his name, your lifestyle will convey "louder than words" that the One you know and love is Jesus!

How can we live with convictions, yet not be considered legalistic? Allow your walk with God to be as natural as having him physically in your presence. Let others see that you pray, and let them hear what words you express when you pray out loud. Aim for using the same words in public as you use in private when you get angry, reprimand, goof, or are caught off guard. Even getting up in a theater or changing a television show because of improper material is a conviction. Walk in the way you would see yourself walk if Jesus were with you! And remember, that "walk" should include more than a list of "don'ts." Be sure to include lots of laughter, affirmation, courage, joy, and encouragement.

Mixed Message #4: Assume that others understand what you mean when you use Christian jargon.

Never assume that seekers understand Christian jargon. In fact, they not only misunderstand it, they also usually don't think very highly of phrases such as "born again," or other religious words like *saved, charismatic, sanctified, salvation,* or *pentecostal.*

When talking with others about your faith, try to put yourself in their shoes. Ask yourself, "Are they rich, poor, young, elderly, or culturally different?" Make your Christian experience earthly for others, rather than so far away from reality that they are turned off. Be gentle, not demeaning. More than likely they don't understand something that you take for granted.

And if, or when, someone ever asks you what it means to be "born again," perhaps your best option is to tell them the story of Nicodemus in John 3! Tell stories, analogies, and parables in order to make your spiritual insights relevant to them. Choose with discernment what phrases or concepts are appropriate when sending cards or letters. For example, if you tell them you are praying for them and you wish them luck, what mixed message might they receive? Consider each encounter you have with a seeker a step toward their ultimate goal of knowing God, and let that influence your words and actions.

COMMON SENSE

If we are making common but unnecessary mistakes, or giving mixed messages about Christianity, we've become a detriment to the process of spreading the Good News of Jesus Christ—*for no good reason!* Common sense, study of the Bible, and preparation take very little extra effort, and they make for an effective, excited evangelist.

Remember, in daring to share your story with another, (1) look for a hook of common interests as your discussion starter, (2) know what you believe so that you can accurately represent the Christian faith, and (3) avoid any common mistakes or mixed messages that serve only to confuse, rather than encourage, your audience.

ELEVEN

Successful Follow-Up

*The primary qualification for a missionary is not love
for souls, as we so often hear, but love for Christ.*
—VANCE HAVNER

I have no explanation for my conversion. Becoming a Christian was completely opposite to everything in my personality and lifestyle. My only earthly explanation is Ralph.

Ralph was the first person I ever met who was really in love with the Lord and spoke with authority about God's Word. He convinced me that there was a great love, healing, and forgiveness awaiting me—and he would not give up on delivering that message until I had given my life to his friend, Jesus.

It took a perfect stranger—a church janitor—who was unashamed of and in love with Christ to introduce me to him. And oddly, I've never had the opportunity to ask Ralph what was at stake for him, for only three short months after my conversion, I never saw him again, nor did I remember his last name or keep up with his whereabouts.

JESUS LOVES YOU!

So the questions linger: Why did he reach out with spiritual comments and invitations to such a hard and cold young woman—and not give up? Why did he attempt to share Jesus Christ with me, when no other person had tried before?

My guess is that he was less worried about my response and more concerned about filling an obvious need. He apparently did not care what I looked like, because I certainly didn't look like a clean-cut candidate for Christianity. He was not dissuaded by how lost I was, or by how unlikely a person he was to attract my attention or affection for his friend, Jesus. None of those excuses or rationalizations stopped him.

His most influential statement to me, the one that actually sent me racing to a church basement closet that desperate day, was, "Jesus loves you just the way you are." How could he have known that six months after we had met, I would come to a point in my life where I was certain that no one who knew me loved me, and even worse, that I did not deserve anyone's love? How could he have known that these were precisely the words I needed to hear? What an appropriate and Spirit-led statement he had unknowingly made!

Ralph had found the key to me. I needed to be loved. I needed his Friend. I needed a Savior. He knew I needed the love of Jesus. He cared long enough to make Jesus known to me.

Before my conversion, I was repulsed at times with Ralph's "uncool" appearance and choice of clothing, but apparently not so much that I would be hesitant to search him out in my moment of greatest need. His sincere love for the lost and for Christ must have compelled him not to give up on me.

SETTING THE PACE

I became a brand new person, a new creature in Christ, when I prayed that "sinner's prayer" with Ralph the janitor on August 26, 1976. It was evident in my countenance, in my appearance, and in my words and deeds.

Ralph's influence upon me didn't stop with my commitment prayer. He invited me to church regularly, took me to (weird) Christian gatherings and introduced me to many of his (odd) Christian friends. He showed me how to read the Bible and find things in it. He even bought me the whole New Testament on tape. He helped me to find an apartment for rent that would allow me to start fresh and apart from my former friends and previous commitments to them, and he helped me to turn from the temptations that came with living with them. He would call me at work—just as I was having doubts about my new life—and offer a timely word of encouragement or give a Scripture reference for me to put my hope in. He never let up until he was sure that I was "hooked" on his Friend—for life.

Without my knowing what he was doing, Ralph set the pace for my growth. He was consistent and thorough in his follow-up of me as a new Christian. He was patient, but stern. He kept an appropriate distance but was never too far away. And Ralph's personal love for Jesus, a love that he freely discussed with me, was intensely real, deep, exciting, trusting, and dependent— no matter what situation or circumstance arose. I a forever grateful for Ralph's love for Jesus. It not only saved my life, but also prompted me to desire his style of evangelism.

Because of Ralph's example, I became the kind of Christian that even Christians don't like to be around— the kind that talks about God with every stranger they meet! I shared Jesus with my co-workers at the car dealership by inviting them to Bible studies, rather than to a party at my house. Many came out of curiosity; most felt I had had a nervous breakdown. They simply could not understand how I could have changed so radically in one day.

I told my boyfriend about my changed life as soon as he returned from a two-month camping trip. I genuinely expected him to be so happy for me—for us! But he said, "Becky, Christians are weak people." I was never so devastated. I had no idea that I would lose my boyfriend, the person I was sure I would marry, because of Jesus. But it was too late. I could not go back to my old life. I had been forgiven of so much that my loyalty and love for God had grown very quickly and deeply. I could not pretend that my new relationship did not exist. I had to go on and so did he. We went our separate ways.

FOLLOWING UP

Ralph taught me everything about successful follow-up. He was always there for me when I needed him. He didn't pressure me, but he never abandoned me, either. He was a true "brother" to me, even though I resisted picturing him in this role.

I haven't always been as successful as Ralph in my

own follow-up efforts. Mistakes are inevitable, it seems, if you are going to share your friendship with Jesus with others. But you can increase your effectiveness as you follow them up, if you are willing to observe a few rules:

- Approach and address others in the same way you would like to be approached: gently, respectfully, pleasurably, inquisitively, and confidentially. Do not be arrogant or demanding.
- Regard others as more important than yourself (Philippians 2:3). If someone views you as being conceited or impersonal, they will not be drawn to you.
- A happy, smiling, friendly person represents Christianity more favorably than a grumpy, angry, impatient person. In fact, friendly people represent *any* organization or cause more effectively!

Now to the biggies . . .

Reminder #1: You don't have to be in ministry or have gone to seminary to effectively share your faith.

Wherever you may have gotten that idea, quickly dispel those thoughts with a brief visit to the New Testament. The early Christians convincingly communicated *who* had changed their lives, *how* he had done it, and *what* they had to do in order to accept it. They were men and women who had witnessed Jesus, spent time with him, grew to love him, and reached out for others to join with them in knowing him.

Certainly, some people are *specifically* called to a

public evangelistic ministry, but all of God's people are his mouthpieces—if they will just accept the call!

Although you do not need to graduate from a seminary in order to share your faith, each of us needs to accurately handle the Word of God, know what we believe, and have a vibrant, personal relationship with Jesus. To be on the cutting edge in our faith, we need to read the Scriptures regularly, receive spiritual teaching, and grow steadily.

Reminder #2: Your neighborhood is a perfect place to share Christianity— especially with your children's friends.

In one neighborhood in which we lived, a friend of my son's happened to be of a religion other than Christianity. In the beginning, we invited Joey to go to church with us. But after a few visits his mother refused to let him join us, because our differing religions were so opposed. But the boys continued to play together regularly.

Because my husband and I feel strongly about not using slang, cuss words, or sharp demands, such as "shut up," I seemed to be constantly reminding Joey that "we didn't say those words in our home." But as the months progressed, I even overheard Joey telling one of his friends who had come over to our house, "You're not allowed to use those words here."

My husband occasionally talked with Joey about God and Jesus. But we walked a fine line. We wanted to respect his beliefs, but still share truths about Christianity so that he would understand why and where we believed differently. After each of these talks, my husband would also explain to our son why Joey's religion was not Christianity, but how it was important for us to plant seeds of truth.

After one of those talks, we didn't see Joey for a while. Meanwhile, we decided to move out of the neighborhood. Jake, who was feeling sad about the change, asked if Joey could spend the night. He never had stayed over before, but under the circumstances, we agreed. Little did we know how important this night would be.

The boys settled into bed and we turned the lights off. My husband and I had gone into the family room to watch TV when we overheard our son ask Joey, "Would you like to pray?"

Our ears perked up. We lowered the volume of the television.

"Dear Jesus . . ." Jake started.

Joey immediately interrupted. "Jake, you know I don't pray to Jesus."

Wow! What will Jake say? I wondered.

"Joey," Jake asked, "do you believe that Jesus died on a cross for our sins and rose from the dead?"

So much for the prayer! Joey said, "Jake, you know I don't."

"Then what do you believe?" Jake asked. During the next half hour the lower and upper bunks buzzed.

Everything my son had ever learned in sixth grade Bible class seemed to be brought into the discussion! I was completely amazed and proud that my son knew how to share his faith so clearly. And he knew that his relationship with Jesus Christ carried the responsibility of sharing what he knew with his friends—that they too might have an opportunity to experience new life on earth and for eternity!

Joey did not make a decision for Christ that night, but now he knows how to—if he should ever have the desire.

Witnessing begins in your own backyard, with the Barbaras and the Joeys of the world. As this story shows, even your children can be a witness to their friends.

Reminder #3: You don't need to know the answer to every question seekers might ask of you before you tell them about God.

Someone once said, "You only need to be a step ahead of the one you are teaching." As a baby Christian, I shared my testimony, tracts, and verses with all of my non-Christian friends. As I grew in my relationship with Christ, I became aware of denominational differences and Christian jargon. I noticed that certain words, verses, and ideas conveyed different ideas to various people. Eventually I found words that were more generic in expression, allowing me to share freely with the majority of people that I met without freaking out some or angering others unnecessarily.

This takes practice! Much of your expertise and style will come through failure. You will find what works with certain people—and what doesn't.

My approach with anyone I have just met is not to tell them everything I know about God and Jesus right away. Instead, I find out where they are in their spiritual journey and take them at least one step closer to God.

If every Christian were to see themselves as planters and waterers along the way, I think we'd get a lot more work done for the kingdom.

When you're sharing your faith, you'll meet every-one from atheists to New Agers, from back-slidden mainliners to people who were baptized as a baby. Wherever they are, never feel as if you have to take each new person you encounter ten steps. Just help them take at least one step in the direction of Jesus Christ.

Sometimes someone will ask you something you don't know or can't answer. This happened to me recently, and I've been a Christian for sixteen years now! When it happens, get a phone number or address where they can be reached, research the subject, and send the information off to them. You might even add a little note explaining that you are always growing in your faith and knowledge of God and his Word—then they will see that Christianity involves a lifetime of growth. All this shows a genuine concern for them. In addition, your answers should be truths that are in the Bible, not doctrines of your particular denomination.

THREE STEPS

Consider your neighbors, friends, family members, co-workers, employers, employees, and service attendants as the people in your life with whom you are called to share your faith.

Can you do it? Let me assure you: You do not need to have a degree or a title in order to tell your personal story to others. But I encourage you to take these three steps when you share your friendship with Jesus:
• Prepare with prayer
• Dare to share your story
• Follow up with care
You'll be amazed at just how many are waiting to hear what you have to say.

TWELVE

Persistent Prayer

*Then Jesus told his disciples a parable to show them that
they should always pray and not give up.*

—LUKE 18:1

It was another person's
prayers for me that taught me the value of persistent
prayer.

I have a prayer partner named Kinney who has
prayed with me for years. She has prayed for my
speaking tours, for the people I have met, and for my
spiritual growth. Then, one day, she told me that she
was praying for my relationship with my mother.

Although both my mother and I had been Christians since my conversion in 1976, our past dysfunctional ways of relating to each other had continued to
hamper the development of a fun, loving, mother-daughter relationship. At the point Kinney talked to me,
I had almost given up thinking that our relationship
could change. Little attempts at spending time with my
mom without getting upset seemed to fail. I had begun
to withdraw and was not trying to pursue a closer

relationship. No matter how many attempts I made or what good intentions I had, every time we met our tone of voice, quick tempers, and old habits got in the way of healthy mother-daughter bonding. In fact, my anxieties about what may happen when we were around each other made me want to stop spending holidays together.

But my friend, during every phone conversation, would remind me that she was praying for healing in this area for me. I would often laugh at her faith, almost discounting the possibility that the relationship with my mother could change. I wanted a good relationship with her, but it seemed impossible.

SENDING FLOWERS

I knew that the tension between us was very difficult for my mom as well. Then one evening she called. She said, "I'm not doing very well . . ." She told me of an incident with Grandma, then how she had reinjured a disc that had caused her pain years earlier.

Mom's vulnerability caught me off guard. *If this was someone else calling me to tell me this, wouldn't I offer to pray for them?* I asked myself. I realized that I wanted my mom to feel better; I didn't want her to be sad or hurting. I must have been harboring unforgiveness if I had not been willing to think these thoughts before.

I offered to pray for my mom. And as I did, I sensed the Holy Spirit prompting me to lift her up, encourage her, and care for her. When we were finished praying, my mother was crying softly. This whole "healing" experience was something new for both of us.

The following morning I did something I had never done in thirty-some years of being a daughter. I sent my mother flowers—and immediately called my friend Kinney to tell her that her prayers were being answered.

But that was just the beginning. The true confessions and honest conversations that followed were difficult for both my mother and me. The flower incident was simply a catalyst that prodded both of us to realize that we wanted and needed to have a healthy, Christ-centered, mother-daughter relationship. Getting there, however, was going to take work and some confrontation.

THE TRUTH OF THE PAST

Over the next year, my travels brought me back to the same Hunter home where I had been a young girl and teenager. Late one evening, as we sat at the kitchen table, we began to talk.

"Why," Mom asked, "do you make our home life sound so terrible when you talk about it and write about it?"

Our eyes met. The air was thick with unspoken thoughts and accusations. She really wanted an explanation, and I felt she deserved to have one. But I knew she wouldn't like the explanation I was going to give her.

For many people, including my mom, the truth of our past is terribly difficult to face and accept. Part of the reason I experienced a fairly quick recovery from alcoholism, I believe, was because I admitted early in adulthood—rather than denied—my alcoholism, my abusive language, my immorality, and all the other many addictions that I was daily involved with. The admission then—at age twenty-one—allowed me to identify with being a new creature in Christ. It impelled me to find help and healing within the church. And though it was painful, discussing my addictions openly from the beginning has allowed me to use my testimony as a tool for alcohol awareness, recovery, healing, and evangelism. Instead of keeping my past a deep, dark secret, I confronted it and dealt with it.

For a long time, however, my mother had denied the truth of the past. But on this particular night, the one thing I had been waiting, perhaps wanting, to hear was that our past was true. I needed to hear her say that she was sorry for the screaming and yelling and hollering of those days. I needed to hear that our home had been dysfunctional, but that now we could go on as a new and different kind of family. I needed to hear that even though we had missed many years of being loving and gentle and kind toward each other, we could still learn to care for each other because of our relationship with Christ.

As my mom and I sat at the kitchen table in our robes at 2 A.M., we looked at the tears in each other's eyes and touched each other's hands. Her pain and sorrow were real, but now that they were out in the open, they were finally subsiding. She told me the things I needed to hear, and something about her sincere confession told me I could trust her love. We made a commitment to care for each other and work at communicating with each other. We cried some more. We laughed. We prayed.

DON'T GIVE UP

You might be thinking, *It took fifteen years to get to this point of healing?* Yes, it did—and that healing is still going on. I might have given up if it weren't for my friend's persistent prayers and insistence to expect healing. I also felt deep inside that every daughter wants to love and be loved by her parents. Like many other people, I had lived with dysfunctional behavior that destroys relationships, homes, and healthy self-images. But my prayer partner, Kinney, taught me a truth to learn and apply to my past—a truth that came through in spite of my past. That truth was this: *prayer changes things!* Long-term, persistent prayers can heal old wounds, transform difficult relationships, and bring us to greater spiritual maturity. So if you've been praying for someone or about something for a long time, *don't give up*. In fact, you may need a prayer partner, like I did, to pray over the long haul. But don't stop praying. God's answers aren't always instant, but he *does* honor the prayers of the persistent (Luke 18:1–8).

THIRTEEN

Open Door, Insert Testimony

The fact remains, when we pray for others, somehow it opens the way for God to influence those we pray for!
—THE KNEELING CHRISTIAN

The doorbell rang. *Oh, no,* I thought, *an impending interruption!* I was in the midst of a hectic summer day, trying to keep track of my roaming junior higher and my schedule as an aerobics instructor. I answered the door out of breath to let the person on the other side know that I was already out of time—before we even began.

At the door stood a young college student. She was athletic looking and friendly, and she wore a crystal around her neck. Those three ingredients caught my attention and piqued my curiosity enough to slow me down to listen to her pitch.

Her name was Kelly and she was selling books, educational volumes kind of like an encyclopedia—not the type of book that would usually interest me. But before I knew it, I had voluntarily invited Kelly and her partner into my kitchen. I knew I was too busy, but I submitted to the full presentation on why her three-volume set of self-help study books would be "perfect" for my child and me.

Somewhere in the conversation she asked me what I did. I told her that I wrote books and taught aerobics, thinking she would ask more questions. But she didn't.

The girls looked a bit frazzled, their brows sweaty and their hair frizzy from the heat of the mid afternoon summer's sun. I offered them a cold drink, and they heartily accepted my offer. But finally I had stalled long enough. The time had come to make a decision. Should I buy the books or not?

I decided that the least painful way of escape at the moment was to tell Kelly that I couldn't make this purchase without the approval of my husband. "Could you come back?" I asked.

"Of course!" she replied. "What time would work best for you?"

We agreed on Monday night at 8:00. Relieved, I put the appointment on the calendar. And then I immediately forgot about it.

The following Monday, promptly at 8:00, the doorbell rang. Who could that be? Jake was at a friend's house, and we weren't expecting guests. In fact, I was enjoying a rare quiet evening alone with my husband.

I opened the door. There stood Kelly, with a huge smile. She was alone this time.

Oh, no, I thought, *I've never even mentioned this to Roger!* So, in front of Kelly, I had to quickly explain in my most inspirational tone why she was there and that I had asked her to present her product to Roger. I got "the look" from my dear husband, but it was relatively congenial and almost condoning. After fifteen years of marriage, he is accustomed to my getting into things like this.

We invited Kelly into the family room and started small talk about college, her home state of Michigan, and aerobics. She was a great salesperson; in fact, I decided I was more impressed with her style and personality than with the books.

My husband politely sat through the complete presentation. At the end he said, "Becky, I don't see a need for these books, but I will leave the decision up to you."

Oh, great! I thought. *Thanks, Roger. Now I have to decide!*

I looked at Kelly and wondered why I hadn't shared my faith with her yet, even though we had dropped a few hints about our ministry with high school kids and our Christian family values. I couldn't put my finger on it, but I had an ever-so-slight intuition that if I were to purchase the books, that would be the beginning of something more. So I said, "Okay, Kelly, we'll get them. Let me get the checkbook." Roger just smiled and nodded in approval.

The very minute I returned to the family room, Kelly spoke. "You said you write books. What kind of books do you write?"

Open door, insert testimony! For the next hour— and we had already talked for at least forty-five minutes—we had a wonderful conversation about God.

It started out as I shared my story of how I met Jesus. She listened intently. Then she said, "I grew up Catholic. I can't say that I know at all what I believe about God."

I had known that already. To me the crystal was a

dead giveaway that she was confused about what she believed.

"But," she continued, "if I were to *want* to learn about God, and know him as you have talked about, where would you suggest I begin?"

"By reading a book!" I exclaimed, thinking that since she sold books and believed in them as tools for learning, she would accept this. "The Bible would be a terrific book to read while you are here this summer. Do you have one?"

"No," she replied.

Then Roger took over. The teacher and gentle evangelist that he is, he shared some basic principles and concepts that would get her on the right course—and he even gave her his personal *Life Application* Bible. I added a few ideas on reading the Bible as if it were a letter from someone you loved, and treating Jesus' words as if they were personally directed to you.

I gave her a Bible and some other books and tapes and left her with a challenge. "Kelly," I said, "if you read through the New Testament this summer, when you return to deliver our books, I'll give you that aerobics video you were interested in."

She agreed. Before she left, she thanked me and said, "I think this appointment was more for me than for you!" I just smiled and mentally praised God.

STARVING COLLEGE STUDENT

One August afternoon I opened the mail. A note said that Kelly would be by to drop off the books. I had been praying for her every day—for her salvation, and for her to understand God's Word. So I was excited to see her again.

The next day she came by at 3:50 P.M., and I had to take Jake to a 4:00 tennis lesson. "Kelly," I said, "any chance you can come back—say, at 5:15?"

"Sure," she agreed.

"Thanks," I said. I could tell she was a top-notch sales person; she was flexible, accomodating, and pleasant to work with. I really liked her!

On the way to the tennis lesson I had a thought: A starving college student at 5:15 might accept an invitation to dinner. So I said to my son, "Jake, please be home at 5:15 for Kelly to show you how to use these books, and then I'm going to invite her for dinner."

"Okay, Mom," he said. (What a great kid!)

By 5:45, we were sitting around the kitchen table— our little family and Kelly—sharing pasta, cantaloupe, and a freshly tossed salad. And I've got to tell you, I've never had *so* many compliments on a dinner before. You can really hit big with any meal if you invite hungry college students.

During dinner, Roger again talked with Kelly about the Lord, using his gentle way of evangelism. He answered her questions, and I could tell she was impressed with his gentle, yet strong godly manner.

Finally I asked, "Kelly, how'd you do on your Bible reading?"

She smiled. "I only got halfway through. But I've never read the Bible before, and I really like it!"

She was returning to Michigan the next day, so I said, "Well, then take it back to school, and when you finish reading the New Testament, write to me and I'll send you the video."

"How will you know if I've done it?" she asked.

"Well, just write to me," I answered.

"You mean, you'll trust me?"

"Of course!" I was charmed by her questions. Then I said, "You know, Kelly, I really believe God has brought Christian people into your life this summer." She had told us about another Christian couple she had met. Knowing she was low on funds, they had offered to change the oil in her car before she left for Michigan.

She blurted, "I know! It's wild!"

We hugged. Then we exchanged addresses and said our final good-byes. She was going home to Michigan, but I promised to keep in touch—and to pray for her.

WILD THINGS HAPPEN WHEN YOU PRAY

Kelly was right. The way God works through his people *is* wild! And the great thing is, he can use *anyone*.

Some people think that I don't have any trouble witnessing. After all, I'm a speaker and evangelist. Witnessing is my job, right?

But perhaps you have noticed by now that I have not shared any evangelism stories from my speaking engagements. Instead, I have purposely focused on people I meet who don't know me as a Christian speaker—the people I see in the hotel, on the airplane, in the bus, and in the daily routine of my life.

When Kelly came to my door, I wasn't "on the job." I could have easily said, "Sorry, I'm too busy to talk to you"—and I almost did! But the crystal she was wearing alerted me to the fact that she was spiritual, yet searching. With an extra nudge from God, I found myself inviting Kelly into my home.

Kelly and I didn't get into a conversation about spiritual matters the first time we met, but God used circumstances to bring Kelly back to my home. And this time, we *did* discuss the Lord, and we gave her a Bible. We even promised to pray for her. And we set up ways to follow up with her—even from a distance. We did all these things not because we were "on the job," but because we love to share our love for God with others. And it was evident that the Holy Spirit was our partner all the way, showing us when and how much to tell Kelly.

Once you start praying, staying alert to the people God sends into your life, God will begin to use you, too. You don't have to be in ministry. You don't have to be a full-time evangelist. All you need is a willingness both to know God better and to make him known.

But watch out. When you start praying expectantly, be prepared—because wild, even wonderful things will begin to happen. My encounter with Kelly was just one more example of how "wild" God can be. For evangelism is as simple as this: prepare with prayer, dare to share, and follow up with care.

Because I have seen firsthand how prayer can turn into evangelism opportunities, and because I believe prayer to be both a natural and exciting way of life, I'd be crazy *not* to pray—and so would you!

Dear Lord, my prayer is that you would create in me a deep desire to know you better. I want to take the initiative to have an appointment with you and I trust that time with you will encourage me to share my love for you with anyone you bring into my life. I ask that you would give me opportunities to grow in my knowledge of you, as well as giving me the boldness and courage to share what I have learned. Please make me into a proud ambassador for you! I love you, Lord.

My appointment with the King will be ...

My neighbors and family who need to know about you are ...

A book that I could read or class that I could attend to increase my knowledge of you is ...

If you would like more information on Becky Tirabassi's ministry and/or her other books and videos, write to her or call her at:

My Partner Ministries
P.O. Box 9672
Newport Beach, CA 92660
1-800-444-6189